The Horse Rode Me
An Afterlife Treatise on Drug Addiction and Reality

Second Edition

by

Bill Marshall

with

David Marshall

Copyright © 2019 by Bill Marshall

All rights reserved

This book, or parts thereof,

May not be reproduced without permission.

ISBN-9781798662960

Cover design by Jessie McAvoy

Other books by Bill Marshall
Gideon McGee's Dream
One Year Short
The Nature of My Game
The Frog Handled Mug
The Blueprint of Reality

"Everywhere I sense a presence, or atmosphere, or atmospheric presence that is well-intentioned, gentle yet powerful, and all-knowing. This seems to be a psychological presence of such stunning parts, however, that I can point to no one place and identify it as being there in contrast to being someplace else.

"At the risk of understating, this presence seems more like a loving condition that permeates existence, and from which all existence springs. The feeling of safety is definitely connected here, in that I know that no evil or harm can befall me, that each of my choices will yield benefits, and that this loving condition upholds me in all of my ways.

"As in life I was always aware of an underlying melancholy, I am here always delightfully conscious of an extraordinary sense of safety that leads, say, to heroic acts and courage—naturally. There is the constant feeling that the universe is with me, for me, and with and for all others at the same time. Not only does it not conspire against me but, it ever lends its active support.

"This willingness to help is everywhere apparent and promotes, of course, a sense of ease that, at the same time stimulates the personality's abilities in ways most difficult to describe. ... All theological and intellectual theories are beside the point in the reality of this phenomenon. "I KNOW that this presence or loving condition forms itself into me, and into all other personalities; that it lends itself actively to seek my good in the most particular and individual ways."

The Afterdeath Journal of an American Philosopher: The World View of William James by Jane Roberts

Dedication

The Horse Rode Me was created both in sorrow and in joy; sorrow for the suffering of the world, and joy for the mere fact of Being. It was created to validate the lives of all of you, but in particular those who suffer from addiction and have come to believe they have no value. This is for those who feel they have in some way failed their loved ones, and for the loved ones who feel they have failed themselves and the ones they love. May the Horse Rode Me bring to all a semblance of peace.

1)

v

The Horse Rode Me

The Horse Rode Me

David Marshall. Our Beautiful Boy...an obit   April 5, 2017

Those of you who knew David know his sense of humor and so I start his obit with his last joke on me and his mother...his dog Barrett. I am 72 and Sarah is 67. Barrett has the energy of a nuclear explosion. He's big, his bark cracks glass and he understands the word 'no' about as much as I understand Swahili. But...he is the most loving dog I know and hasn't a mean bone in his body. He is a sweet boy. But, Damn, David...really? So on to the obit, which I would like to give the title: Beautiful Boy, which is a book by David Sheff. David is our beautiful boy and during his darkest of days, this is why we never abandoned him. Never gave up on him. Never.

As a child, David was much like Barrett. Turn your back on him and he was gone. Curious about everything. "I wanna see. I wanna see." Always said twice. Always. His hair was platinum blonde then and fine as silk. Now it is Viking red. Funny how that works. Sarah loved long hair and so David, as a child, had long hair. He wore it like a Samurai pony tail, until when in the 2nd grade the class bully taunted him about it. Sarah got the call. He punched out the bully and made him cry. David was fearless. He eventually became friends with the bully, and the bullying stopped. This was our beautiful boy.

By 4th grade he was reading Stephen King. All of Stephen King. There should have been a clue in that, but we didn't catch it. David's intellect was apparent early. He was built for our system of education. If he read it he understood it and remembered it. Learning came easily for him, and so he flew through school.

The Horse Rode Me

Soccer was his sport and as a child his team was one of the best in the state, but for most of his teammates, burnout set in and deprived NFA highschool of a treasure trove of talent. I was a runner and so he entered my world of cross country. He had good cardio and as his mother likes to tell him...about many things..."it's genetic." These things made life easy for David, but in time he chose the most dark of journeys. It was within this journey that David learned non-judgment and most importantly, compassion. Having experienced the deepest level of judgment and loathing he chose their opposite.

His intellect, curiosity and athleticism is not what made David our beautiful boy. What made him such has been reflected in the hundreds of messages sent to Sarah and I on the effect David had on those he touched. Through everything our beautiful boy was kind, compassionate and open to everyone. If you were struggling, he was there for you. His laughter was infectious and his smile seemed more warming than the sun. I suppose his mother and I instilled the basics, but his dark journey taught him how powerful acceptance, empathy and compassion can be.

When he came out of his darkness and back into the light of the living we had our beautiful boy back, risen like the mythological Phoenix from the burning cauldron. He knew the history of those that entered the cauldron, all for their own reasons. They bring something back, but the fire is always close behind. David's legacy are those he has touched in a way that may have changed them in ways they are not yet aware. The physical symbol of that legacy is a loving community he started with his friend Josh. That community is Crossfit Payback. You have become the living symbol of David's spirit. Determination, strength, acceptance, compassion and inclusion. These traits are my Beautiful Boy. He is physically done here, but the seeds he has planted in us will grow...if we tend to them. TEND.

Written by Dave in 2010 (age 23). Two years before getting clean and seven years before his death.

The Horse Rode Me

I have experienced every facet of the "disease of addiction." Before I started using I was confident, proud, happy, and very driven. When I reached the pinnacle of my use I was depressed, filled with shame, weak, and deceptive. I hope to make my way back to that first list, but I know I have a lot of work to do.

When I become obsessed with something, particularly getting high, I've found that I become a person that I don't really like. I become very anxious and agitated, and I cannot stop thinking about it. The thought consumes me, and when it comes to getting high, I can become very crafty in how I overcome this obsession. I've made up lies to get money and the drugs.

When I'm completely filled with the obsession to use, I will act compulsively without considering the consequences. If I have a little clean time under my belt, and I'm thinking sanely, then I act like an adult and weigh out the pros and cons. The self-centered part of my disease has made many of the people close to me resentful and distrustful. It has made friends and family think I don't care about them, and that I'm a full-blown narcissist. My family doesn't trust me to act in my own best interest, or theirs. This has made me depressed, filled with regret, and I've felt and feel very guilty.

Drugs made my face and back covered in scabs and scratches, and I went through the most intense physical withdrawals a person should have to go through. I became mentally weak, and caved in to all my cravings no matter how big or small. I didn't have any spirituality, didn't see the beauty in pretty much anything, and rarely thought of anything other than myself. I also became emotionally numb, and didn't really feel anything when I was high. My mind was on cruise control. When I wasn't high I was going through such intense withdrawals that the only emotion or sensation I felt was pain and sadness.

Most recently I gave into my self-centered drug addict ways and used six days ago after I was fired from my job. The only unhealthy obsession in my life is with opiates. It has ruined relationships, and made me very resentful towards myself.

A Letter from Jill Bertolini, read at Dave's Celebration of Life 7/21/2017

I am so sorry I am missing David's celebration of life. I know how much he loved all of you and how much he loved Payback. Had I been able to be there…this is what I was hoping to share,

I met David in 2014 when I reached out to the Crossfit Payback owners to see if they would be interested in coming to Rushford Rehab to speak to my clients about health and wellness. At that time I had no idea how deeply connected David was to helping people struggling with addiction. I met him for the first time in the lobby of my building…instantly he was all smiles and had a ton to say. I gave them a quick briefing on what speaking to a room full of 42 clients can sometimes be like. Prepped them on a few key points they should focus on and then walked them into the room full of 42 clients. They each told their story, David was second. David made them laugh, some cried, but by the end he had 42 clients and countless staff completely adoring him. He was raw and he was real. We all loved him.

After that I asked if they would be interested in coming back every few weeks to run a "gentle" Crossfit style workout with my clients. David instantly said yes and that is what he did. Once a month he drove to Rushford to run a group. While it was meant to be a workout, it always turned into some sort of therapeutic discussion. Sometimes he and I would co-facilitate the group. I would be "therapeutic" and he would be "real."

This is what I wanted to share with you. Being able to get to know David through that type of venue was such a gift to me. I heard his story countless times, but each time something new would resonate

The Horse Rode Me

with me. He shared joy, he shared pain, he shared embarrassment, he shared fear; in the room with them he was never afraid to tell them how much he feared relapsing. He made it something okay for them to talk about. He knew it could hit anytime and he knew the inevitable dangers of a relapse. They would ask him "if you still worry about relapsing why did you start your own business, why bother?" This is where he shared his greatest gift of all...he shared hope. He would tell them that he isn't living for a relapse, he's living for himself. No matter how many times I heard him talk about his hope, it took my breath away every time. He would tell them how much he loves the man he's become and how hard he had to fight to get there. He told them he had no regrets and that all of his ups and downs made him who he is today. His message was always the same, "I going to be better today than I was yesterday, and better tomorrow than I am today." David inspired hope. David challenged them to grow, and David made them feel accepted. For all of their flaws, their pain, their crimes...when he spoke to them he accepted them for the person they were in that very moment.

That's the David I know and love. All he wanted to do was help. Whoever, whenever, where ever. And that is what he did. And it was always about help. When I was going through a painful point in my life, I found refuge at Payback with David. He made me laugh, he made me cry and he accepted me. He accepted me for all of my flaws, all of my pain, all of my crimes. He challenged me to grow and he inspired me to be better. Isn't that what he did for all of us? He challenged us one way or another.

David loved and cared about everyone. But I have to say...if he let you into his heart he loved and cared about you fiercely and loyally. So much so, that when it was time for him to let us help him, he couldn't stop helping us. I can tell you that he did not want to let anyone down. You were all so very important to him.

There is a saying I heard somewhere I now use constantly...There are three purposes that people come into your life; a reason, a season or a lifetime.

The Horse Rode Me

Jill Bertolini

Spoken by Emily Hancock at Dave's Celebration of Life 4/17/2017

I met Dave Years ago and every time I saw him it was a smile and a genuine hello. But I didn't develop the friendship that'll forever be part of me until about three years ago. It was in the gym, before anything was here that Dave talked about his ideas to build his community. Bare walls, no mats, no weights, but just him and his eagerness to start this new chapter of his life. Steve and I had just come home from St. Maarten, newly engaged. One of the first places we stopped was here. Dave, of course, welcomed us with his huge smile, hugs, and a congratulations, and three years later Steve and I were lucky enough to have him in our wedding. The gym is where our friendship truly began. There wasn't a day that went by that Dave didn't come up in conversation, not a day that a text or a phone call wasn't made. I felt like I had known Dave my entire life. And as we all know, that was the type of person he was.

He fit in instantly with all of us, and I often wished that he had come into my life many years prior to this. But I am beyond grateful that I had 3 wonderful years of his friendship. It was always the five of us...me, Steve, Ben, Em and Dave. Every single weekend it was us, always the five of us.

Jeans, Datin Dave, Dancing Dave, habitual line crosser were some of the many nicknames we had for Dave. Each name earned, up until he met the love of his life, Becky. We retired the nickname after that because Datin Dave had officially called it quits. He loved Becky so much, and we do too. It's hard to put into words the love I had for Dave. When you're blessed to experience a friendship like the one I had with him, words don't seem to do it justice. He was caring, empathetic, intelligent, genuine, a free spirit and absolutely hysterical. Dave and I talked about everything. There were no filters and usually Dave was always crossing the

The Horse Rode Me

line with his jokes, which he thought were hysterical. The hand on the chest, head pushed forward with no sound because he was laughing so hard. Which was always contagious. So many laughs, all the time, no matter what. If Dave was there, we were laughing. The many nights hanging out at Ben and Em's sitting around shooting the shit, sitting by the fire, laughing, talking about life and watching music videos. Dave was obsessed with watching Grace Potter singing, I Shall be Released, and now more than ever I understand why that song had more meaning to him than I realized.

Weekends away, hiking, taking the dogs out, swimming, working out, my family parties where he was always the one dancing with all the ladies. These are the times that are forever engrained in my mind and the memories that I will forever hold close to my heart. He was the type of friend that could instantly make you feel ok, he brought me back to reality many times when my mind would get the best of me. He was wise and always thought outside the box. He had a way to put things into perspective, always reminding me to live in the moment and not to worry about the things I had no control over. And if anyone knew how to do this, it was Dave. And even when Dave was struggling, he was always concerned about how it was affecting others. He cared more about the people he was hurting than
at times he did himself.

I find myself saying "God damn it, Dave" daily. God damn it that you're not here. God damn it that I can't see you, hug you, laugh with you. God Damn it that I couldn't do more to help save you. God damn it that you weren't able to live the long beautiful life you deserved. In his short life, he affected more people than most do in their long lives. Dave had such a beautiful soul, much credited to his parents who loved him so deeply. All I can do is hope that Dave is finally released, and hope that he felt and knew how much he was loved.
Emily Hancock

Emily, me and Becky…always laughing

The Horse Rode Me

Introduction

You might be wondering how I could be writing this book in the voice of my son David, who passed away on April 3, 2017 of a heroin overdose. Considering your current beliefs about reality and death your curiosity and doubt is well placed. So, I want to try to make sense of it for you. In 1988, during my 43rd year and one year after the birth of David, a series of events occurred that led me to question the nature of reality itself. My understanding of it stopped making sense to me. I began remembering all of my dreams and learned how to interpret them. I read everything I could get my hands on about the nature of consciousness, including quantum physics, religion, out of body accounts, psychology including the collected works of Carl Jung, mythology (specifically Joseph Campbell) and stories of remembered reincarnational lives and near death experiences. What came of it all was a fundamental restructuring of my belief systems regarding life itself, much of which I shared with David. Our conversations began in 2001, shortly after he turned 13, which we celebrated with a Native American sweat lodge ceremony along with three of my closest male friends.

One morning when David was fourteen he came downstairs in a state of great excitement. Because we had previously discussed the topic of out of body consciousness I suppose he was somewhat prepared for what happened to him. "Dad," he said. "Last night as I was falling asleep my mind left my body. I was in my room watching myself fall asleep. I was literally not in my body. I got a little scared and as soon as I did I was back in my body."

I share this with you here as an example of the pliability of David's mind. It was incredibly porous and open to new experiences and concepts. His drug addiction was four years away.

The Horse Rode Me

It was a good time, filled with hope for the future. David was brilliant, handsome, personable and physically gifted, the perfect cocktail of traits necessary to fulfill the "American Dream."

Skipping ahead to 2015. David had been clean for three years. I was at work when our office nurse, Deb Boyle, approached me in my office. She seemed hesitant, but plowed ahead with what was on her mind. She had been with us for six months. She said she felt comfortable sharing what she had to say in that I would probably be open to hearing it. She told me that she is a "sensitive" as I recall her description of herself. You may know the term as a psychic. She can see and interpret energy of the departed, and told me that there is an energy field of someone who has passed following me around. It turns out that it was my best friend, Steve Hancock, that died of pancreatic cancer in 2006. She told me things she could not possibly have known about my friend Steve, and that he wanted me to contact another of my friends, who Steve said was struggling. That she was able to do this and that the ability to do it existed did not surprise me in the least.

Fast forward to May of 2017, a month after David passed. Deb had moved to Florida a few months earlier, but before she left she told me to call her anytime. My wife, wanting assurances that David was Ok, felt that now was the time. Among the many things she told us, she was adamant that David wanted me to write a book about heroin addiction. He said it was important. There were many books already in print about heroin addiction and written by people far more expert in the field than I. It was not a topic I felt comfortable writing about and so I didn't. She also said that David wants me to know that, "I was right about everything." I had an idea what he was referring to and that it was connected to the book he wanted me to write, but I couldn't be sure at the time. I suspected it was about all the information I shared with him about my understanding of reality.

In June of 2018 my wife Sarah and I were preparing for a trip to Topsail Island, NC where we spent many vacations with David and

The Horse Rode Me

Jessie when they were children. In my previous conversation with Deb Boyle she told us that David would like some of his ashes dispersed in two of his favorite places. One was on the hill where he grew up in Yantic, Connecticut and where we still lived at the time of his passing. The other was Topsail Island, North Carolina, where we vacationed for several years when the kids were little. Some of his ashes had already been dispersed in the center of the Burning Man bonfire in Nevada by his best friend Zack. My memories of Topsail Island run deep. David and Jessie would scream with delight when I would throw them over the waves with their butts hanging below the inner tubes they floated upon. There was nothing about those years that could have foretold what the future would eventually bring.

Sarah began making a Viking ship to launch into the ocean in which we would place a vessel containing some of David's ashes and light it on fire. I called Deb to have her contact David to update us on his thoughts. He liked the idea of the Viking ship, but again strongly reinforced his previous comments about writing the book. At the least, I decided, I would bring my laptop to Topsail Island and see how I felt about beginning a book in a place that was so important to David and to me. Topsail Island seemed the right place as it was where I wrote my first book, Gideon McGee's Dream.

We arrived at our rented beach house on Saturday July 14, 2018. After unpacking our vehicle I stepped onto the beach for the first time in nearly twenty years. The feeling of David's energy was palpable. In my head I heard the words, The Horse Rode Me. It was the title of the book I suggested David write soon after he got clean in 2012. I knew in that moment I would write David's book and that his energy would filter through me into the words I typed into the laptop. What you are reading in this Forward is the only part of the book that I directed consciously. That is to say that the content of the book came through David's energy that enveloped me as I wrote. I had no idea which direction the book would take. I merely sat at the keys and waited and went with whatever and

The Horse Rode Me

wherever David guided me.

I end this small contribution to The Horse Rode Me by sharing what happened with the launch of David's ashes. Sarah made the ship out of many layers of paper mache and coated each layer with waterproofing. David's sister, Jessie, did the artwork. It was a ship worthy of its intended task. From bow to stern it was three feet long and one foot wide with a dragon head rising above the bow and its tail raised high above the stern. It was just before dusk that we headed toward the waves. I had loaded the boat with flammable materials such as paper towels and fire starter blocks then saturated it all with lighter fluid. I went first into the waves with an inner tube around my waist and one of those lighters with a long stem wrapped in a baggie and stuffed in my pocket. My best friend Tom Lee, who had shared David's sweat lodge many years ago, followed behind holding the ship above his head so as to avoid getting it wet.

Our struggle to get the ship beyond the wave line was dicey. The ocean was rough and the undertow strong. But we made it. I removed the lighter and its waterproof baggie from my pocket. Tom was treading water holding the boat steady. The lighter worked, but attempt after attempt to light all that combustible material failed. It should have exploded in Napalm-like flame. A rogue wave eventually filled the ship with water. I removed the cloth bag in which David's ashes resided and emptied it into the ocean. I looked down and David's ashes swirled around my body embracing me, as though intentional, in a love I had not felt before. And then it was gone. I reached over and pushed the ship under the waves and made my way back to shore along with my buddy, Tom. I thought I had sent David's Viking ship to Valhalla. After all, it was made of paper mache and should have been torn to pieces by the strength of the ocean.

By the time I made it to shore there was a bit of excitement on the beach about 200 yards from where we stood. David would not allow that ship to burn, and to our amazement would not allow it to

The Horse Rode Me

be destroyed. After pushing the ship to the bottom it had somehow surfaced and rode a wave into shore completely intact. It came to a rest at the feet of a family down the beach. Tom ran to them, told the story of the ship and David, and returned with the ship fully intact. The symbolism of all this was not lost on me. I dried off, entered the beach house and opened my laptop. The Horse Rode Me began its entrance into our reality.

The Horse Rode Me

The Horse Rode Me

Hi! I'm David

All of you at one time or another have uttered the words, "I wish I knew then what I know now." I felt those words at the moment of my death. First of all, let me assure those of you that fear death that there is nothing to be afraid of. It is simply the end of one moment and the beginning of another. A step sideways, so to speak, neither up nor down...if you catch my drift. I realized at that most auspicious moment that I had played the game of life with a near-total lack of understanding of what the game was about and how to play it. My father was 40,000 words into this book when he read a post on Facebook. It was from a book he had read several years ago. I sent such a strong impulse to him that I wanted our book to begin with that specific quote, as it encapsulates nearly everything I will be sharing with you here. He has become quite facile at feeling my energy and my direction in composing our book. All of you have felt a similar energy surrounding you when a loved one of yours had passed. Jane Roberts, the author of the book from which the quote was taken, is acknowledged by many as one of the greatest 'sensitives' of all time. She is a person who is sensitive to energy that originates from a dimension/reality that is not yours...for now, but is as close to you as your own breath. It is a similar action to what my father and I are engaging while creating The Horse Rode Me. The words are his, but the direction of the book is mine. Through him I will share with you NOW what I wish I knew more fully THEN.

The Horse Rode Me

As my father mentioned in the forward, I first contacted him through the 'sensitive' Deb Boyle and let him know that "he was right about everything." In your terminology I literally shouted to him through Deb that he had to write this book. It took some wrangling to get him to do it. The Viking ship that would not sink was the clincher. Much of the information he had already incorporated into his life, and shared with me while I was still alive...as you refer to it. Basically, the book unfolds like this. My father sits at his laptop, quiets his mind and allows my energy to mix with his and direct the flow of the book, not the words, but the flow. I come through to him as feelings, intuitions and impulses. Since, as you will discover in reading this book, we are all connected as ONE, and because my father was open to it this was not difficult for me to do. He had no idea in which direction the book would go and so you will find no chapter headings, but rather idea headings. So, Let's get started.

Years ago, after I got clean and before I relapsed, my father suggested I write a book and call it The Horse Rode Me. Horse is his generation's name for heroin. Funny name for a killer...my killer. Add the letter 'e' to heroin and the word becomes a female hero. Take away the 'in' and it becomes a male hero. I like that, for heroes and heroines are exactly what the heroin epidemic is about. My father couldn't have known at the time how appropriate that title was, or that I would be directing the writing of it through him. But timing is everything as they say, and as I have discovered, timing is never wrong. Bad timing, good timing. It doesn't matter. The timing of things is always right, always perfect. It simply doesn't conform to your faulty ideas about control... or time...or of reality itself for that matter. I know this now, but I sure as hell didn't know it then. Then is when I was still alive...alive as those of you who are still breathing, and eating and shitting and crying and laughing and loving...and suffering.

You can believe what you want about how my book is being written. But, the fact that you are now reading this is no accident, for, as you will discover, there are no accidents, no mistakes, no

The Horse Rode Me

one to blame, including yourself. You drew my book to you as surely as gravity anchors you to the ground and you drew addiction to you just as shit draws flies. There was purpose to it. The mere reading of this book will change you. Your beliefs will throw up many arguments against what I am going to tell you here. My answer to your arguments is a question. Look at your life and look at your individual and collective history, then tell me how well what **you** believe has been working out for you. Tell me this; if you knew how to reduce or even eliminate much of the stress and trauma you experience throughout a lifetime, wouldn't you do it? How do your beliefs about victimization and accidents and blaming serve you? My guess is that you do not appreciate being a victim or having an accident, and both take the responsibility for your life off your already weighted down shoulders and place it on another's.

My journey with you ended by way of a heroin overdose that was tainted with Fentanyl. You are probably only one point of separation away from knowing and loving someone who has died from an overdose of heroin. One point of separation is an epidemic, and epidemics are powerful symbols, an outer expression of a shared inner knowing. Addicts are the soldiers of the symbol, the heroes and heroines of the heroin epidemic that is trying to tell you something. In a manner of speaking they have thrown themselves on the grenade so that you might wake up...not to the epidemic, but to who you truly are. You have all learned from us, even if you don't yet realize it. The thousands that have already succumbed to this scourge know this as I do, and many of my friends are here with me. Of course, I didn't know it when the Horse was riding me, sucking me dry as sure as a vampire drains its victims of blood. Heroin use is a devil's bargain, a false prophet, an orgasm that once acquired becomes harder and harder to reproduce. I remember all of it. Heaven and hell wrapped up into a cooked liquid that had to be shot into veins that became increasingly more difficult to find and to hide. Our arms, too visible to non-users, become our shame, and so we often find other, more hidden locations, to poke holes through our flesh, or

The Horse Rode Me

wear long sleeves in Summer.

Why am I writing this, you might ask? "Why do you give a shit about what happens to the rest of us?" you ask. "You've done your suffering, kick back and enjoy the peace, the peace you were looking for, but couldn't find while you were alive. Your battle is over!" I give a shit because millions still suffer. It is only now that I feel the full force of the connectedness that I only guessed at when I was suffering with you. I write this in the hopes of breaking the spell that heroin or any other addictive substance has caste upon you. I write this to break into shards the methods currently used to break that spell by good, well-meaning people who also suffer simply by the weight of their failed attempts. The pain of that failure, I have since come to understand, is as great as the sense of abject failure felt by my addicted brothers and sisters. I write this for those who have loved me and still love me and wonder if there was anything they did or didn't do that could have changed my own outcome. There is a paradox in the 'cause' of the heroin epidemic. Individually there is no one or no thing that is the cause of another's choice. One can be an influence, but never the cause. Certainly, there was no individual or thing that caused me to use heroin for the first time. There was only misplaced curiosity. Collectively, however, everyone on the planet shares in the cause. You have created a world of separate parts that has become an epoch set on eternal repeat. A madman playing Sim Earth couldn't have done a better job of screwing it up. When a drug can create a better reality, false as it may be, than reality itself, it should set off some major alarms. I'm sounding the alarm by telling you who you really are and why you have chosen to be alive in a physical reality. I intend to challenge virtually everything you believe about who you are and how your reality works. All I ask of you is a temporary suspension of the beliefs you hold, if you have any at all, regarding who you are and why you are here. But first I want to share with you who I was before I side stepped to where I am now; and yes, it is merely a sideways movement. I'll do that by sharing with you some of my journal writing and letters from friends and family. Everything in a different font is direct from my journals

The Horse Rode Me

and letters. Standard text is my commentary.

Age seven:
Dear Tooth Fairy,
I lost my tooth and it did fall out so you still have to give me the money.
From,
David Marshall

It appears money already played a central role in my life by the age of seven. A definite impact of the American culture. I couldn't forgive the tooth fairy her debt to me.

(What follows is my trip to Paris with my uncle Dave and my sister Jessie. I was twelve years old.)

Dear Journal
April 13, 2000
Paris is awesome! We went to the Arch de Triumph, W.H. Smith, And I actually saw the Eiffel Tower! Well anyways, when we first got to Paris, it wasn't what I expected. Then we went looking around and it was more than I expected! I got 1,018 francs I exchanged for my money, and I still had $2 left. This lady, when I was buying a post card, I think was making fun of me in French,(because I didn't speak French,) We also looked for this photo gallery with a bunch of naked women pictures for about an hour. I wish there was some more stores that was more my style. I also went on my first subway. They smell like crap!
Talk to you tomorrow,
Dave

Dear Journal
April 14, 2000
Today was definitely a shopping day. Although we went to

The Horse Rode Me

Notre Dame Cathedral. I got an Adidas watch for 450 francs. It's the best watch I have ever had in my life. This Japanese lady grabbed Jessie by the arm and put this red and brown fake hair thing in her hair and practically forced her to buy it, which she did. This lady that sold something to Jess was really hot. She was selling Jess this cool hair thing. The best part about today was hangin' out with Jan. She was funny. Her little son Branton [1 yr 4 mo] was really cute and funny. He was fun to hang out with; I would have him for a little brother. She also started to breast feed and I've never seen that before but I didn't care. I just didn't look. Well, I'll talk to ya tomorrow.
    Dave.

Dear Journal
April 15, 2000
    Yesterday was fun. I got this French soccer jersey. It's really cool. We also went to see a movie called Girl Interrupted. It was about the story of a sane girl in an insane asylum. It was a great movie. We also went to the French Army Museum. That was really fun. We saw Napoleon's tomb there. My favorite part about it was the armor. They even had armor for kids that would fit me! So today was fun! See Ya!
    Dave M

Dear Journal,
April 16, 2000
    Today at 9am we went to see Versailles. Louie XVI lived there. The fountains were the best part about the whole thing. There was music and everything. At 12:45 pm when we got back from the trip we went out to eat and it tasted pretty good. My sister wanted to get their rip off junk toy thing. It cost like 60 francs. After that we went to see Jim Morrison's grave even though his body is really in Oregon. I got my picture taken next to it and it was pretty cool. There was a poem, cigarettes and flowers on his

grave. Some people have no respect for the dead. We went to Jan's place soon after and I met her husband Roy from England. We went to this place called Lean's. I had muscles for the first time. They're great. Then we had dessert back at their place. Then we went home and that was the end of our day.

See ya!
Dave

Dear Journal,
April 17, 2000

Today was OK I guess. We went to Jan's house and left from there to go get tickets to London on a train. We have 1st class both ways. Then we went shopping places (none special!) We came back around 4pm or so and had hot chocolate and cookies. I played with Branton for the rest of the time. Then we went to the

Eiffel Tower but we could only go to the second floor because the top floor was closed because of huge winds. Well, that's our day.

See Ya!

Dave.

Dear Journal

April 18, 2000

Today we didn't do anything much so don't expect anything long. First we went to the Louvre, but we soon found out it was closed on Tuesdays. So we tried to get into Musee d' Orsay, but the line was two blocks long so we passed and had launch. Then we went to this museum (I don't remember what it was called) that had the statue of "The Thinker." Soon after we went near the Eiffel Tower and got our pictures drawn. They were professional artists and the drawings looked just like me and Jess. We went back to the apartment and rested for a little bit and then went strolling around the neighborhood. We ate out, had Haagen Daaz. We got back around 9:45pm and I went to bed because I was really tired.

Well, See Ya!

Dave M

Dear Journal,

April 19, 2000

Today we hooked up with Jan and went to some shopping stores. We went to the park and Jess and I stayed with Branton. The we all got a little pissed off because there was crap on our shoes and on the baby carriage. Branton went to sleep for an hour after that. We just went window shopping after that. We said goodbye to Jan and Branton and went to the Louvre. We saw the winged something or other, that statue with no arms and Mona Lisa. I don't know what's so special about the Mona Lisa. Half the painting there were better than that. We then saw American Beauty. It was one of the better ones.

Well. Talk to ya tomorrow!

The Horse Rode Me

Dave M

Dear Journal
April 20, 2000
Today we went to London, England on the Eurostar! It was great. We took a taxi cab to go to Harrods. Harrods was HUGE!! They had everything there. My uncle got a tie. I wanted a Diesel shirt but they were too expensive. I also wanted a Manchester United Jersey, but my uncle said, next time. (if there is!) We also went to the science museum. It was cool. There was a lot of hands on stuff and that made it even better. Then we got back to Paris at midnight.
Talk to ya tomorrow,
Dave M

Dear Journal
April 21, 2000
Today was the greatest day yet. We did a lot of window shopping today. Unkie Dave was really nice today.(even though he always is). I got the Manchester United football jersey today (soccer). I've wanted that jersey for a while. Unkie Dave got himself a really nice pen and Jessie a couple good ones. Unkie Dave almost got this really nice painting but he decided it was too expensive. He went into a lot of fancy men's shops. That will be the clothes I wear when I am a Fund Manager. The only bad part of today is that this is the last day NO!!! I have had a lot of fun the past 10 days.
Well, Bye,
Dave

That was a great trip, but what I want you to notice was how much I talked about the cost of things and buying things. "STUFF!" I was twelve years old and already looking forward to being a Fund Manager. This had nothing to do with my parents and everything to do with the culture into which I chose to be born.

The Horse Rode Me

The Horse Rode Me

Twelve Years Later

Dear Journal
January 2, 2012
I am back in another treatment program at MCCA in Danbury. I've been kicked out of two sober houses since November. First for blowing 5 bags and ODing on the Harry Rosen living room floor. Secondly, I did not follow the rules and left Quinnipiac about a week ago. As soon as I arrived home I thought it would be a good idea hit up L...

It was New Year's Eve that my father had to drive me the eighty miles to Danbury for detox. As was my custom I always shot up before going into rehab. Danbury Rehab was one of only a few places in Connecticut that would detox you from both heroin and Xanax. I was too high for them to admit me that night and so we had to go to Danbury Hospital for Narcan and observation. They dismissed me at midnight and we checked in to a hotel before going back to Danbury rehab to detox in the morning. It was not a great night for my father.

Dear Journal
January 7, 2012
As you can tell from just the asymmetrical letters that had dysfunctional and fucked up written all over it, I was still a mess from that last run. I'm not saying I'm better, but I'm a little bit

The Horse Rode Me

better. I left detox today and arrived at the beautiful rehab that is Mountainside. It's a good crew of guys here with a positive energy throughout the group. On top of being blessed with people I get along with, the food here is great, the location and view is even better, and the one roommate I have is hilarious and quite the story teller. I will keep it short though because it's late and I have to get up early tomorrow. 'Night.

God, thank you for keeping me sober today, getting me to Mt. Side and giving me a great roommate.

That great story teller and roommate was Chris O'Connor. A few years later he started the podcast Dopey with his friend Dave Manheim, who also became a friend of mine. Dopey now has over a million downloads and is a great help to active, recovering and clean addicts. I highly recommend it. It's a no- bullshit and irreverent podcast that was right down my alley. Chris relapsed and OD'd in 2018. He wants me to say Hi.

April 6, 2012 97 days clean and sober

I get along with pretty much everyone in the house. When I got down here Mike was the only one I connected with, though. I can tell he's insecure about himself, and I relate to him on that level, but I wish he thought higher of himself. My father would think it's good that I say that about someone else when I have the same issue. Maybe vicariously through one another, and by being good friends to each other, we can get to the level of ease and comfort from within we wish to achieve. I'm done writing for tonight, but I have plenty more to write about tomorrow.

<u>Prayer</u> Thank you for keeping me sober and away from cigs. Thank you for giving me a good day and for helping me do the right thing.

Mike was here to greet me on April 3, 2017. He says Hi.

April 7, 2012...98 Days clean and sober,
This is the longest I've been sober since I was 15 yrs old, and

The Horse Rode Me

it's a very alien feeling. I still fantasize about taking an enormous blast of crack, or shootin' dope, but under no circumstances am I willing to go back to where that blast or shot brought me. It's been quite the journey since I got to Mountainside on January 6, but I know it's only the beginning. I'm just getting to step 2 with my sponsor, and I feel like we're doing good work. I need to get moving on my steps so I can start step 4 when I go to jail on April 27. I'll have plenty of time in there to do a thorough 4th step, but I'm not really looking forward to doing it.

The jail bit was for a second DUI. You do stupid shit on dope. During my several year run I totaled my parent's Ford Focus, had earlier dropped the transmission and later ran their Jeep Wrangler off the road. Luckily (I'll have more to say about luck later in the book) no one was hurt, including myself. I robbed them blind and pissed all the college money they spent right down Alice's rabbit hole.

April 8, 2012...99 days sober
Today was Easter, but by no means did it seem like a holiday or "special" day. That's not to say it was a bad day, but because it was a holiday I felt lonely. It would have been nice to spend the day w/ my family, but Norwich is not the place for me. That's when people, places, things, and the word "Acceptance" comes into play. I think about all of my friends from back home, and I really miss them. They are all good dudes, and support me in my recovery, but they all still get high. When I went home for court last Thursday I saw JR and he was rocked. I hope he can find recovery, because he will lose his new business if he doesn't. I also really worry about Ricky. He has some kind of Illness where he pukes and shits blood, and drinkin' and druggin' is only bringing him closer to the grave. Someone might look at my life right now and think it's gone to shit. I live in extended care, work at a rehab for next to nothing, and I'm going to jail on April 27th, but the funny thing is I'm the happiest I've been in a long time.
Wake up.

The Horse Rode Me

Accept the grit,
Accept the shit,
Embrace the great.
Happiness.

Prayer Thank you for another day sober. Please help those still suffering find the rooms & recovery. Relieve me of the bondage of ego self so I may better THY WILL!

My father once told me that four times more young people from Norwich died from drug overdoses than died in the Vietnam war. That number continues to climb.

April 9, 2012...100 days sober
I've been really looking forward to getting my life back on track lately. I know I'm supposed to live in the moment, but I can't help fantasizing about the future. Lately I've been thinking I'll go back to school and get a degree in kinesiology or something that would land me in the sport and fitness world. I cannot wait to get my life going again, but I know I need to be patient. Impatience is directly correlated to my disease, and when I want something, I wanted it 5 mins ago. If I don't stay sober and continue doing what I have to do Then I'll achieve nothing and end up back in jail or dead.
Hope and Patience!
Prayer Thank you for keeping me sober. Thank you for helping me do the next right thing.

April 17, 2012...108 days sober
A lot of shit has gone down since my last journal entry. The thing that hits the hardest is that Carl Armstrong is dead. He overdosed like so many of my other friends, and it's so tragic & unnecessary. I related to Carl on such a deep level. I saw the same pain, despair, emptiness and hurt in him that I felt within myself. When he was doing well, he became a beacon of light. You could see so much hope in his eyes when he was sober. I wish he could have found recovery and gotten sober, because not only did he

deserve it, but it hurts to think how much he could've brought to this world. Other than Carl's death, I'm also dealing with having to go to jail in 10 days. On April 27th I'm supposed to go in for 60 days, but I'll hopefully do less. I'm very nervous, and I really don't want to do it. I feel that the judge could just see how well I'm doing here, he would just mandate me to stay at Mountainside. I know that's not gonna happen and I'm just gonna go to jail. Just being stuck in a cell ALL DAY is going to drive me crazy, and that's the scariest part. I'm gonna need your help with this one God.

I'll also have more to say about God. She and you are bigger and more powerful than you think.

On top of all this I also found out I have Hep C. It's just so fucked up. I HAVE HEPATITIS C. Are you fuckin' kidding me? What was I thinking when I was sharing needles with C.....? I really need to straighten this shit out & do whatever I have to to get rid of it. And even talking about C.... still gets me a funny feeling in my gut. I just care about her so much, and I'm so scared she's gonna die. How do people like her and I make it through so many overdoses, and others die with their first one? I know I don't have another run in me, and neither does she.
<u>Prayer</u>: Thank you for my life and all of my blessings. Please help me come to terms with the consequences of my actions. Please help C....find honest recovery and happiness.

Prophetic about not having another run in me. I should have reread my journals before relapsing. Maybe not. As you say, it is what it is. I know how true that is now.

April 30, 2012...121 days sober.
I can't believe I've been HONESTLY sober for this long, but I also can't believe I was getting fucked up for as long as I was. Sometimes, I'll get a flicker of a craving, but I've really been able to hold onto the way I felt in the past and use it to overcome

those cravings. There is just no worse feeling than having a dull needle shooting cocaine for hours on end with it stabbing yourself repeatedly because you can't find a vein, bleeding and puking all over the place, then realizing you have to go into work in 20 minutes. Killing myself was a viable option when I ran out of a large supply with no benzos or heroin for landing gear. Nowadays my biggest problem is which girl I'm gonna go after, or which one thinks I'm hot. It's all shit to feed my ego, and to verify to myself that I'm the man. My ego really does run wild and get outta control, but I think my recognition of it is a step in the right direction. I'll find myself thinking that I'm better looking than any other guy in the room, and that every chick wants me. Writing that down makes me realize how ridiculous I am lol.

Thought for the day: Does writing about drugs and women tell me anything?

Prayer: Thank you for keeping me sober and nicotine free. Thank you for my friends, both alive and dead who keep me sober.

I was incarcerated at Gates Correctional Facility in Uncasville, CT. for four weeks from late May to late June. The word 'Corerectional' is a joke. Punishment would be more apropos. What follows are letters to and from me while in Gates.

5/26/2012
Hi Dave,
Just a short note. Put $50 into your acct. via Western Union. It will still take some time to set up phone service – have to fax them our last Comcast bill -then 3-5 days for them to process. Called Jason – he's more than willing to help with getting your probation transferred to Salisbury, CT. He wants you back in the house, but I'll need to pay – no problem. He's concerned you have to be in Norwich for 3 weeks. I told him I'll drug test you, which he appreciated. I guess Pete is struggling – Jason will ask about Ebay.

I'm heading up to Pittsfield, MA in about 2 hours. Half

marathon tomorrow. Oh, I put your address on your FB page. We're all hoping this experience will help you stay sober. Keep your head up and your Monkey Mind under control. We all love you. Mom will see if Jim (Chelle's husband) could use your help when you get out. All will work out,
    Love,
    Dad

You'll learn much more about the Monkey Mind later in the book.

5/27/2012
Dave!
Holy Crap. I miss you. I saw on Facebook they are keeping you longer than expected, and I know when I was in Jail I never got any mail and wish I did. I love you to death. You've helped me more than you know. You are such a strong, positive and lovable person. I messaged you before I heard the news, but I'm coming to Millerton! I'll be there in less than two weeks, so when you get out
   we definitely need to meet up. I don't know how long you will be locked up, but I know you will do just fine. Your personality is so vibrant and people are drawn to you – in a positive way. Stay strong and driven, which I'm sure won't be a problem. If you haven't shaved your mustache by now you might want to consider it...unless you want some creeper envisioning you roller skating in an American flag Speedo down the boardwalk. I've been in contact w/ Frat Matt & James and we are looking to reunite a family dinner when we are all in the area, so get ready for it because it's going to get <u>real</u> weird, might invest in a pair or two of Depends. Just know that you are an incredible person and a beautiful person inside and definitely outside as well. You are so loved. I cherish the time I had at Mountainside with you. You were always there for me and I could tell you anything and everything and that meant so much to me. More so that you felt

you could share with me as well made our friendship tighter. So be good and I can't wait to see your crazy self soon!
Wolfpack love,
Becca G
5/29/2012

Dave,
What's up Brother!!! How are you doing? We all are sending our love from up here. I miss talking with you Bro. Can't wait till you get out. How's that fourth step coming? Haha. Sorry...Bad joke. Couldn't help it. Just spoke with your Dad and got the address and contact info for you. Sooo...He said you have to go home with a bracelet on your ankle!! Gay!!! Anyways – since you can't go back to NY with the monitor – maybe you could go to Don's house since it is in Canaan Ct. Don said that's an option. He has 2 beds open and I left a message with your Dad with Don's contact info – Don said it's cool for you to be there with the bracelet and can do whatever the Court needs to get you there. So you're in a good sober community and we can bust out the work we have been doing. So any help we can be we are here for you and we love you Brother! Write me back anytime and I hope all is well. AND KEEP YOUR HEAD UP – you're a sober child of God – and God doesn't give us anything we can't handle with his help.
Love you brother,
Keep up the good work,
Michael S

I'll have some first-hand ☐ information about God later in the book. For those of you that 'believe' in God it may surprise you. Look for it toward the end of the book.

5/30/2012 (from my sister)
Hey Dave!
How are ya holding up? I know you're in there longer than you had expected/hoped, which sucks, but I know you can handle it.

The Horse Rode Me

Good thing you like to read & workout. Plus, if you are there for 30 days, then you are more than half way done! ☐ Anyway, I've been busy "wedding planning" and making cakes. Dad and I ran the half marathon this past weekend. It was <u>so</u> hot and hilly! Our time was 2 hrs 5 mins. Not what I had hoped lol!

If I ever do another half it'll be on a flat course. Dad won his age division though ☐! Also, Doug came in fourth overall in the full marathon and was the first Berkshire County finisher! We missed you, so you'll definitely have to come next year! Except Dad and I will prob do the 10K instead haha. So are you going to train for a triathlon? Yeah, so our wedding is coming in less than 3 months! Seems like there's still so much to do! Invitations, ceremony, music, favors, seating charts, etc. Weddings are so expensive! If you ever get married, go to some tropical island or something haha ☐ Anyway, hang in there Dave! I'm so HAPPY & PROUD of how well you are doing, & I KNOW YOU CAN KEEP IT UP. Once you get this sentence over with you can put it all behind you and focus on your future (because the past is the past).

Okay, see you soon.
Love you!
Jessie

Hi Jessie!
What's going on?! Life is fuckin' awesome on my end! LOL. Well, not really, but it's not that bad. The first week in here I was on lockdown 23 hrs a day, and had nothing to read or write with. I've been in the gym for the past 2 weeks, and it's a lot better. There's a pull-up and dip bar and I get to watch TV, so it's alright. Mike D'Andrea is here with me too lol. It's nice having an old friend in here though. The last three weeks have literally felt like a lifetime. I CAN'T WAIT to get out! They barely feed you anything in here, so I'm always hungry too. I get commissary tomorrow though. The time will go by a lot quicker when I'm not hungry every waking moment. Anyway, that's awesome that Doug came in 4th in the marathon. Tell him I said, "FUCK YEA!" lol. And 2:05 is

a good time for the ½ Jessie. You should be proud of that. Most of the sloppy disgustingly fat Americans don't even know what a half marathon is. Landing on the moon is more realistic than running 13.1 miles to most people. Lol. Don't count yourself out for next year just yet. Remember that you're a Marshall, which makes you a thoroughbred champion. We win, that's what we do, lol. I guess that's it for now! Thank you for writing me, and I love you so much.!
Love,
Dave

5/30/2012 (from my brother Tyler)
Dave,
Let me start off by saying I love you. More than you can ever know. I was 14 when you were born, so you're more than a little brother to me. You're in a place now that I've spent years in. There's no lessons to be learned there except not to go back. I don't know what you're feeling or how you're doing, but I desperately want to know. I don't know what else to say so please please write me back. My address is on the envelope.
Love,
Ty

I've always loved you, Ty. I was always proud of you, even during our mutual madness. Know this, there is meaning and purpose to it all.

5/30/2012
Hi Dave,
I mailed the stuff you sent me to the probation office and gave Jason the probation officer's phone number. He said he'd call. I also filled him in on what's going on as well. Everything will work out – trust! I'm at work now, it's 9am Wednesday. You may be just waking up after your post-breakfast nap. Hopefully that $50 is available by now. Not much drama – if any -going on. Grateful for

The Horse Rode Me

that. You may know that Zoe (our mini Dachshund) is deaf. It doesn't seem to bother her, though. She still begs and whines as usual and demands that we lift her onto her couch, but only in the evening. Maybe she runs out of energy by then. She's getting pretty old and grey in the snout. Earl and Ed – being cats – let nothing bother them – a great trait that we humans can take a lesson from. Oh, almost forgot. Jason had to ask Pete to leave the house. All he would say was that Pete was struggling. Sorry, I know he is your friend, but then we can never control another's choices, nor are we ever responsible for another's choice. On a high note, I'm as cute and clever as ever.

Love,
Dad

5/29/2012
Hey Sweetie!
Just a little note to tell you I'm thinking of you and Love you!!! I got this card in Hawaii long ago – as you can see the envelope stuck to it. Thought the photo of the girl was beautiful and it would be nice framed. Never did though. It really sucks that the 4 day thing didn't happen! Don't know why they would tell people that. Dad said you looked and sounded good. I hope you are and it's not too awful!! Hopefully in 2-3 weeks it will be over and you can put it all behind you and begin your <u>new life</u>! We missed you this past weekend. We were up with Jess and Doug for the marathon. They did great. Dad and Jess ran together and Dad got 1st in his division – over 60! Doug did great – 4th overall and third male finisher. I guess the course was horrible. Lots of hills and it was really hot. When Jess got home from the race she wasn't well – nausea and headache. She didn't drink enough and was paying the price. They had a 5 and 10K too, so next year Dad and Jess will do that Instead. Maybe you can run with Doug!! Dad said you are reading a lot and working out a lot too. That's good. Do they have a decent amount of books? Are the guys there being OK to you and the guards? Hope so! Can't wait to see you and get you back

up to the Berkshires!!! I love you Dave and will write soon.
Love,
Mom.

6/1/2012
Dave,
I'm seeing Tyler tomorrow and I hope things are OK. He has no job yet but did say he has a girlfriend. I'm planning on accepting him "as is" although old patterns of "wanting to fix and save" are strong. We all choose what it is we wish to explore in this particular life of ours, so who am I to judge what another soul has chosen? This, of course, includes you. It is difficult though, seeing someone you love suffering. Maybe some day the human race will feel that way about all mankind and not just those they love. Blah, blah, Blah! ☐ Hope to see you soon,
Love,
Dad

This is an important point my father makes here. It is called Acceptance and I will get into it later in the book. I'll also be addressing Choice, better known to many as Free Will.

Until my relapse, nearly four years later, life was good, or good as I defined the word while I was alive in the flesh.

August 1, 2012....7 months sober

It's been 3 months since I last wrote anything, and I'm boiling over the top with negativity. First, let's recap the last few months. I ended up staying in jail for four weeks instead of four days. I stayed in Norwich for a month on parole; had to lie about where I'm living in order to stay at J's house, and I'm barely working at all. I also have Hep C and I'm pretty sure I have Lyme Disease. The first four months of my sobriety was a cake walk. I stayed busy, was happy most of the time, and enjoyed myself. I guess the pink cloud of early sobriety is finally wearing off.

The Horse Rode Me

The Horse Rode Me

The Horse Rode Me

Four Years of Sobriety

After my "correctional" prison experience and a short stint in Norwich I returned to Millerton, New York, just across the northwestern Connecticut border. I was staying in a sober house run by my friend Jason Sherman, a great and compassionate guy with a sense of humor similar to my own...twisted. I had been in two other sober houses prior to getting clean at Mountainside Rehab in Canaan, Connecticut, and let me tell you, I might as well have been staying in a flop house. They did nothing more than reinforce my feelings of self loathing, feelings that you all need to overcome. The corridor between Millerton, NY and Canaan, Ct was a special place for me. There was a large and supportive sober community, the geography was spectacularly beautiful and life was good, as you would define 'good.'

I worked on a farm mucking cow shit and at one point aided in the birth of a calf. I eventually moved to waiting tables and was pulling in pretty good money in tips, not fund manager money, but my wants were few. During a brief one month stay in Norwich, CT after release from my correction I hocked up with my eventual gym partner Josh and it was then that I fell in love with Crossfit. I taught regularly at a gym in Millerton before deciding to move back to Norwich and open a Crossfit gym we named Payback. I had no thoughts of ever relapsing, but we both believed we had much to atone for and thus the name Crossfit Payback. I'll have more to say about atonement later in the book.

The Horse Rode Me

Josh and I opened Crossfit Payback in April of 2014 after months of cleaning, painting, building, sweating and bitching. For me it was a birthing experience. Everybody helped, but special thanks go out to my mother and father and brother Tyler, and to Josh's father. It was the kind of grunt work that kept me going because of the vision at the end of it. Life opened up for me. The gym was busy. I was busy...and happy. I truly cared about life again. Making friends was always easy for me, maybe because I cared about them. I had my own apartment, met the woman I loved, and traveled and competed in Crossfit. The skills that I will be sharing with you in this book were something I did not have, but things were going the way I wanted. Who needed skills when life was good, and why does it turn to shit? Addict or not, you understand what I am talking about here.

Rushford Rehab in Middletown, CT October 2016 Journal notes
Day 1 10/17/2016 I was high when writing this first entry, as I always got high before entering rehab. A last hurrah like giving up cake and bingeing just before the quit.

First thing my father accuses me of getting drugs outta the car, when in actuality it was pens, a checkbook and a couple other things. I'll be heading to Rushford today. I can't believe I'm back in this spot again. I'll write more later. I'm tired. I miss B.
Part 2: I do not miss detox AT ALL. This place fucking sucks. Everyone is so edgy and they have me on clonidine, so I feel incredibly weak.

CLONIDINE SUCKS
Barely walk,   weak, zombie-like, still feel dope sick. They flushed all the dope out of me at the hospital Saturday, so I

passed for opiates. I have track marks everywhere because I shoot dope. I'm about to lose it. IPT better be better or I'm fuckin walkin. **YOU HAVE NO FUCKING IDEA WHAT MISERABLE IS**. I am truly miserable right now.

Let's look at the effects of clonidine on the body (blood pressure med) A: Dormant red blood cells. B:Dormant red blood cells don't leave, or slowly leave the left ventricle to oxygenate the blood slowly. C: Slow brain function as a result. D) Slow oxygenation throughout all body cells. E: Fact that w/out oxygen nothing is possible, no cell metabolism, no cell perfusions.

*I HAVE LOW OXYGEN LEVELS FROM FLUID IN THE LUNGS.

Next Day 10/18/2016

No luck in getting methadone. Is a high dose of Clonidine safer than a high dose of methadone? Absolutely not. Everyone is sitting here staring at movies they've watched a thousand times to numb their minds the same way the substances they used got them here. One kid tried to tell everyone in the room that A) Einstein is stupid. B) Theory of relativity is wrong. C) Quantum mechanics is wrong. OH MY FUCKING GOD. I couldn't help myself. I explained that Relativity works for large objects, using an example, and that quantum mechanics also is correct but it takes quantum physics and the development of a TDE theory (Theory of Everything) to explain everything. Back to the main point, I can't take methadone and I'm here for opiate addiction. The fuck? If I didn't have anything to lose, I would fuck up the first rude, inconsiderate person I came across. I'm raging out.

Next day 10/18/2016

I am so incredibly tired, I want out of this detox so bad. I am beyond miserable here. I just want to talk to the people I love. I hope I'm only here for 2-3 days max, because this sucks, man. Why do I do this to myself? Are drugs and alcohol a symptom of the problem or is it something bigger? It is such a strange phenomenon that affects so many people. Is it definitely a genetic predisposition? Is the right question: why do I have this affliction and is the answer 'so I can help others.' I certainly know it has helped me in the past, and it is one of the greatest feelings to help with genuine intention. That spreads to every facet of humanity, though, not just alcoholics. Maybe being alcoholic pushes you into that role much easier than if you're not. However, it includes immense pain to yourself and those around you, and maybe your death. I have NO idea why I started using again. Depression, misery, why was I either. I just want to get through this detox and get upstairs.

10/25/2016 Day 8 @ Rushford
It's so strange being back at rehab... I never thought I would be, yet here I am. So it goes...I'm just going with the flow, and feeling much better than this time last week. It's kind of fucked up but this is the happiest I've been in a while. Just goes to show how getting fucked up all the time can really skew your perspective, and alter your entire reality. I have confidence I'll be sober and successful in all aspects when I get out of here. On that note, time to hit the hay. I forgot to note that the nurse just tried to give me 2 different muscle relaxers before bed, because the Dr. fucked up and didn't give them to me in detox. Anyways, I was honest and turned them down.

10/26/2016 Day 9 @Rushford
-AJ likes fart porn and is serious (2nd WTF of the day). E leaves tonight. Hope I get a good roomie...

10/27/2016 Day 9@ Rushford.
It feels strange without E here now, but it does feel peaceful. Other than that I feel pretty good today. The days are repetitive and monotonous here. It would be nice to have just one day where we could just kick back and do nothing. This sun up to sun down with little to no rest sucks.

11/1/2016
2 weeks sober. Working on not letting J occupy anymore space

in my head, and not letting his bullshit lies get to me. My wind is exponentially better. Looking forward to picking up a barbell again. My new roommate is a 62 year old toothless crackhead named Rodney.. That being said, he seems nice and harmless.

11/3/2016 Sixteen Days Sober
This place is starting to wear on me, and I've felt either just off or depressed all day. I can't tell which. The weight of my reality is crippling at times. I am so incredibly nervous about my future and the future of the gym. The gym is just an extension of me, and the thought of it possibly failing is terrifying. I think this is my last-ditch effort at pulling out all the stops and possibly making the gym's growth explode. The boxing classes and Dean's presence will definitely help. Sometimes I wish I had a normal career where I didn't have to think about work 24/7. My goal is to get the gym to the point where I no longer have these fears and doubts. Or maybe if the gym is just an extension of myself these fears and doubts should be banished by faith that if I work diligently on myself and the gym, everything will pan out. This seems like the best approach I can come up with for now. Time will tell...
I will talk about fear and trust and doubt later. At this point doubt and fear had become a strong habit, one which was far stronger than faith and trust.

11/5/2016 18 Days Sober
My level of irritation when I'm just in the same room as Louis is becoming unhealthy, let alone when he speaks, He's so full of shit.

11/7/2016 20 Days Sober
Been sleeping alright. Rodney wakes me up when he talks in his sleep. Been in a little funk lately. Is it the vivitrol? My brain still repairing itself? Or just Life?
-"If you worryin about what a muh fucka doin, then you, muh fucka, probably gon relapse." Rodney.
-"no doubt." Rodney.

The Horse Rode Me

-Clinician told me it is common for people to feel depressed or in a 'funk' 2-3 days after the administration of Vivitrol. That being said, I feel much better today than yesterday.

11/8/2016 21 Days Sober.
-"Jesus mutha fuckin Christ, I woke up again..." Rodney

11/10/2016 23 Days Sober
-Donald Trump became President yesterday...Terrifying.

I left Rushford a few days later, having no conscious awareness that in less than five months I'd be dead. What I did have awareness of was a high level of anxiety about the status of my future. I had the knowledge of staying present and the benefits thereof, but not the habit of it. My habit was to engage the Monkey Mind. My relapse soon after leaving Rushford was less a physical need for heroin, as it was an overwhelming need to relieve my anxiety.

True First Day Sober...4 Days No Dope
2/6/2017
Even though I'm on Suboxone for now, I am so much happier, and feel so much better than when I'm on that shit. I regret taking those fucking K-pins so much this past weekend. I have to be honest and tell my sponsor. Becky loves me more than I love myself I think. I just wish she loved herself that much. She really is my best friend and the most beautiful person I know. My goal for this year is to stay sober, be 100% honest and grow the business. With J gone the sky is the limit.

Rushford Rehab Middletown, CT. Letters from friends.
10/18/2016
Dear David,
Important things first. I love you. Much love being expressed for you around here. Maybe you'll see that what others see in you that makes them love you, you do not see in yourself. We've

The Horse Rode Me

talked about this. Also, if you remember, we spoke of some of your worst moments occurring right after some of your best days. I think there is a part of you that feels you don't deserve the happiness that comes with great days. If so, and it is probably unconscious, I think it is driven by some demons you hold from some of your darkest hours. You must let them go. It is only your dwelling in the past that keeps them alive. You may want to share this possibility in your therapy session. Mike will keep an eye out for your Husky card. This was an unexpected miracle, a gift from heaven, as it will relieve one major stress in your life...Hep C. So grateful for that. I was quite sure from the beginning that your income level would have qualified you for Husky Insurance. Say Amen! The number you gave me for C was wrong so I Facebook messaged him with your request and statement that you will return stronger than ever. Messages continue to come in on your phone with love and support. Tears well up when I read them. I respond as me and let them know you appreciate your love. Things are being taken care of at the gym. Focus on you. Appreciate something about yourself every day, several times a day. Believe me when I say it is a powerful technique. Stay present and quiet your Monkey Mind.

    Love you – see you soon on visiting days.
    Dad.
    P.S. Barret is good.
    Just got your call. Not a great start.

10/23/2016
Dave!
    First off, we miss you! But are so thankful you've decided to get help. We couldn't imagine our lives without you in it. Our Jeans crew would be incomplete ☐ I wanted to give you this journal to hopefully help pass some time. Whether it's writing, drawing, doodling...whatever. But also the saying on the front cover couldn't be more fitting. "Every morning we are born again. What we do today is what matters most." Buddha. What's done is

The Horse Rode Me

done, and now what matters is how you move forward. We're thinking of you every day and can't wait to see you.
Love you,
Emily and Steve and da Monk.

You make me Laugh harder than anyone else
You bring out my loudest cackle laugh.
You have the best smile.
You have an infectious laugh.
I love the way you kiss.
You make me smile...every day.
You're the strongest guy I know,
Physically and mentally.
I ;love your hands. I don't know why,
I just do.
Your dedication to the fitness of others
As well as yourself is admirable. You're so good at what you do.
You're a people person. There's not one person
That has anything bad to say about you. You're a very good friend.
You're a kind and loving boyfriend.
Seriously. So. Handsome.
You're one of the smartest people I know.
Sometimes it's gross,
But you have a great sense of humor.
You have awesome parents.
You're Penny's favorite guy.
You're my best friend.
Someday you'll make drop dead gorgeous babies, and hopefully
I'll be luck enough to harvest them.
I love your eyes.
I couldn't imagine life without you.
I think about you ALL THE TIME.
Love,

The Horse Rode Me

Becky

Well that was short lived. My relapse continued and the longer it lasted the more insane I became. The EMT service in Norwich and Backus Hospital got to know me by name. I never did anything half assed, including my addiction. Overdoses were rampant during those last months and were it not for my parents and friends keeping an eye on me my checkout date would have occurred much earlier than 4/3/2017. I felt so much guilt over what I put them through it amplified my self-loathing. From my current perspective, however, I understand it all quite differently. You are soon to get to that new understanding, but first a few random undated pages my mother found among my journals and letters. I was high when I wrote the first one.

Ravenous explosion
Skewed vision and a deafening ring
Endless euphoria
Was it real?
Calm after the storm
Styrofoam soul
Disconnected and empty...empty...empty
Is this life?
Awake
God-shaped void
Blissfully present
Returning to the source
I am Alive.

......

"What you have to do
You do with play.
Life is without meaning.
You bring the meaning to it.
The meaning of life is
Whatever you ascribe it to be.
Being alive is the meaning."

The Horse Rode Me

Facebook Goodbye

April 3, 2017

Bill Marshall It is with a heart so heavy I can hardly bare its weight, that I post this on David's page. At 7:30am this morning we were informed of the passing of our beloved son. For those of you that knew him you will understand why his mother and I never gave up on him. He had a light in him that most that came into his life easily saw, and a smile that could light up the darkest space. His humor was…shall I say…different and complex, irreverent, yet never meant to hurt. He had a brilliant mind and his knowledge was broad and deep. But most of all he was a good and kind person. It was this that we loved the most about him. Sadness is not a word big enough to encompass our feeling of loss.

Ryan H: Thoughts and prayers with you. I loved Dave, he helped me tremendously through my struggles.

Marcia M: I'm so sorry, Dave was one of my best friends when he lived in Millerton. He's one of the best people I've ever known.

Bryan K: My thoughts are with your family. Dave was one outstanding guy.

Norma V: I'm just heart sick. It's as though a light has gone out.

Megan K: Thinking of the entire Marshall family. Send strength and love. Dave will be greatly missed.

Michelle W: Love you all so very much. I know that words cannot ease the pain you are feeling. We are here if you need anything. I love you.

M Jean S: I can't get over this news...I'm so sorry Billy and Sarah! Dave was an amazing person and he is going to be missed by so many.

Lucia M: Such beautiful words and the truth! Dave's an amazing person lost too soon! So sorry for all of you.

Andrea L: What a terrible tragedy. My condolences to all of you.

Abby S: My thoughts and prayers are with your family. He was an amazing kind soul who will be greatly missed.

Mary Blair H: I only crossed Dave's path for a few weeks of training a few years back. But I immediately felt his warm heart and took a big liking to him. I'm so sad to hear this tragic news and my heart is with you all. Big big big time.

Mary R: I'm so sorry for your loss. Growing up around Dave I know what a great kid he was. Always happy and smiling and just fun to be around. I really can't wrap my head around this.

Jesse B: You did a great job raising him, everybody loved Dave. He could make anyone laugh and smile.

Jordan J: I didn't know Dave for that long but he was one of the coolest guys I ever met. Always let me in no matter if it was the gym or his house he always welcomed me and never treated me like an outsider. Thanks for the good memories ima miss you man. Look over all of us.

Stephanie D: Your son was indeed a good and kind person. He had a gentle way about him that made you feel at ease when you were around him. I am so sorry...very sorry.

Elizabeth L: Hugs Bill...loved Dave. He was always kind and helpful.

Peter E: Happy to know his legacy will live on through those who he loved and by whom he was loved in return.

The Horse Rode Me

Nicholas M: Dave was a great coach and an even better fried. My heart goes out to you and your family.

Amy G: I am so sorry to hear about David. What a great guy and such a kind heart. He will be missed by everyone who ever met him. My condolences to all.

Joe C: Known Dave since 4th grade. Quick witted. Outgoing person was always helpful to me and I'll be forever grateful.

Anna F: It's hard to believe the man I knew as my so's best friend throughout highschool and then some is gone. My thoughts are with you and your family. I will truly miss seeing his handsome face, exuberant personality and cheerful smile.

Christopher H: He was a great brother-in-law and a great uncle. Love you guys!!!

Jamie B: So sorry for your loss. The world lost a one of a kind, incredible person and he will be missed dearly. Rest easy Dave.

Natalie L: I am at such a loss for words...my deepest condolences to your son and your family. I haven't seen your son in years but he is one soul I will always remember and I will always cherish the memories with him and the conversations we had.

Kaitlyn M: It was impossible not to love Dave, his smile lit up the room and he had the biggest heart. Thinking of you all, I can't even begin to imagine your pain.

Laurie C: I'm so sorry Bill and Sarah. We loved Dave very much. He was such a big part of our lives for so many wonderful years. He will forever be in our hearts.

Eric B: Your son was a smart, descent man. He was taken from us before he could reach his fill potential; which I believe had no limit. The world is a lesser place without him. I'm very sorry for this loss

Virginia L: Bill, Sarah, and all your family, we are devastated by this news. Feeling so very, very sad and speechless. Sending you all our love and strength to help at this difficult time; David. Rest in Peace.

Karlei S: Such a sad sad day. So very sorry for your loss. His smile is one that could never be forgotten. RIP Dave.

The Horse Rode Me

Travis M W: Sooo sorry for your loss and for your family. Your son was a good man. God bless David Marshall. Love you man.

Krista S: I am shocked to hear this news. My heart goes out to your family. Dave was a great person. And that smile-one of a kind. He will be greatly missed. Rest Easy Dave.

Devon C: My heart aches for you and the rest of your family. Dave was a wonderful human being and I was grateful to get to know him. My thoughts are with each and everyone of you all at this extremely difficult time.

Morgan A: I'm so sorry for your loss. Prayers to all you guys. Dave was something special in this world.

Joshua Ryan: OMG this breaks my heart. He was such a great guy. I'm so sorry for your loss. He will be truly missed.

Alex S: I'm so sorry for your loss. The last time I saw him was a little while back just as he and his partner were starting up Payback. He was so excited, so full of life. Before this I hadn't seen him in years but that didn't matter.

Britney K: Dave was such an incredible person. Intelligent, caring, handsome. It was obvious that he was raised in a good home. My heart pours out to you Mr. & Mrs. Marshall. Sending thoughts and prayers that you will somehow find peace in this incredibly difficult time. Dave's bright personality is going to be missed by so many. He will never be forgotten.

Heather F: Sending love to you and your family. You raised a remarkable man.

Dee C: I'm thankful to have known him.

Cameron Lemaire: My condolences Bill. You did a hell of a job raising Dave. He was a really good guy.

Chad D: I'm sure you already know this but Dave loved you and Sarah more than anything in the world and he was so proud that you two were his parents.

Abby S: I'm so sorry for your loss. Dave was an incredible person and always had a smile on his face. He was the kindest person and loved his friends and family so much. The world has lost one of its brightest souls. I'm so very sorry for your loss.

The Horse Rode Me

Brendon E: My condolences to you and your family. Dave was a good friend and will be missed by all.

Rachel S: I'm so sorry. I have so many great memories from growing up in Yantic with Dave. Thinking of you and your family.

Erika C: Love you Bill Marshall! Dave changed my life and being at Payback gave me a family that I will cherish for life! You raised a great man. I will miss him but I will keep going because I know he wouldn't want me to quit! Love to you and your family.

Shawn S: There was always a mutual feeling. Always hugs all around.

Steve M: I haven't commented on much if anything since this all happened so now I would like to express a part of my feelings about Dave. I never had any interest in weights. I could care less about working out with weights. I finally told Dawn I would join Crossfit and do it with her. It was Dave that changed my mind. He made me feel so comfortable starting this journey in Crossfit training. The only person I learned to beat, was myself. One of the most memorable comments Dave said to me was, and this was because I was agitated with the ability of throwing the weight up. "Check your ego at the door." I'll never forget this. I'll miss him always. He taught me a lot. He was such a smart caring young man. We all have our personal experiences with Dave. He was one of a kind. It's just not fair that we all lost him. Just not.

From Chris O'Connor...Co-Originator of the Dopey Podcast
8/1/2017
Dear Bill and Sarah,

It's been some time since Dave's passing and I wanted to reach out once the dust had settled a bit. I seem to process things a little differently than most people. When I learned of Dave's death I was upset, but it did not come as a total shock. Over the years I've developed a hardness around these things, probably out of necessity.

What I did do was insert myself into the situation. I asked

myself what I could have done differently. I knew Dave was struggling and I knew the severity of his addiction. I always took his calls and tried to cheer him up when he was down, but I did not spend time reaching out to see how he was doing. Maybe it's selfish to think I could have made a difference, but it is something that bothered me after his passing and still does today.

The point of this note is not to dump my own feelings. It's to let you know what Dave meant to me…And what he still means. My own beliefs are obscure, but I do hold that Dave is still out there. It comforts me to know that his presence exists somewhere in the ether. I think of him often and even share what is going on in my life – stupid things that I am panicking about or losing sleep over. Perhaps this sounds silly to you, but I wanted to let you know that just because he's gone, he isn't gone to me.

Of the people I've known that were taken early, Dave was definitely one of the closest. I know I will think of him and talk to him for the rest of my life.
Chris O'Connor
(Chris joined me on July 24, 2018)

Enough of Me. The Rest Is for You

The Horse Rode Me

To this point what you have read, many will consider to be the meat of this book. I disagree. It was merely my attempt to open your eyes to the fact that the heroin epidemic is destroying valuable assets to your growing awareness of who YOU are. Most addicts will see yourselves in my rehab journals. They were more for families and loved ones who have little or no idea of the physical and psychological struggles we go through while trying to get clean. What follows are my father's words, sharing what he had shared with me while I was still alive (as you understand the word), and confirmed from my current 'ethereal' stance. I have let him know in no uncertain terms that it is my desire for him to speak as me.

I recommend while reading what follows that you suspend your current beliefs regarding who you are and why you are here. Feel your way through what I am about to tell you. Shut down your chattering Monkey Mind, which loves to tell you what a shit you are and that what you are about to read is bullshit. Its goal is to keep you stuck in the status quo. You believe 'shit' happens. You believe you are victims. You believe others are the cause of your feelings. You believe in accidents. You believe you control some things, but not all things. Most of all you believe that coming into the world was not your choice. So let's start there, at the beginning.

The Horse Rode Me

The Beginning Was a Conscious Choice

In coming to understand what your life is all about you have to start at the beginning, and the beginning took place before you were born. You have learned, and believe, that who you are began at the moment a single sperm cell penetrated your mother's egg and that you had no choice in the matter. Have you not wondered what it was about that one cell and no other that opened the egg to **its** penetration? It almost seems conscious, doesn't it, as though there is purpose to the combining of the specific spermatozoa with that particular egg. Any other sperm cell and you would not be the you reading this book. Any other egg and you would not be reading this book. Was it luck of the draw, random selection, simple coincidence or the hand of God? Those are the easy answers and the ones you believe, when real knowledge hides itself from you, as it did from me. The real scoop is like the elephant hiding in the room and no one can see it. The fable of The Emperor's New Clothes points to our blindness for the obvious. A few years before my final O.D. my father said this during one of our many philosophical conversations, "It makes no sense to me that consciousness arises out of matter, that without matter there is no consciousness. It makes more sense that it is the other way around." That one sperm, accepted by my mother's one particular egg, one specific egg, is what gave me the ability to grasp what my father said to me at the age of 12. It gave me my physical appearance, and the attributes that most suited **my** choice of navigation in a physical world. The selection of that sperm and which of my mother's eggs it would enter was **my** choice, for I existed before my mother gave birth to me, before time itself. Nothing is random. Nothing is a mistake. There is no fate. There is no destiny. Everything is by choice. It is the same for you, all of you.

The Horse Rode Me

Before I was born, I had already selected what I wanted to explore in physical form and what parents would provide the greatest set of <u>probabilities</u> to foster that exploration. Without their agreement I could not have been born to them. Agreements and choices often come from a deeper level of consciousness than mere thinking. You have greatly underestimated the power of consciousness. Your birth, your parents and your physical form and function were all preselected by you and with exquisite precision and purpose. It wasn't luck. It wasn't a mistake. You are not, nor have you ever been, a happenstance or a victim or God's marionette. If you were born to scumbags it was with great deliberation on your part. You saw the probabilities that lay before you in making your exquisitely precise choice. Nothing and no one are the cause of you. You are the cause of you. After those initial selections everything exists as probabilities from which you choose. There is no fate. It is all free choice and you generate your own probabilities. God does not sprinkle them before you, nor does she wield a magical miracle wand. It's all on you. God is so far beyond your current conceptions that you actually limit yourself by way of your current beliefs about who or what God is. You have not the language or words yet to begin to describe what God is. You have merely made god into a grandiose and often bellicose version of yourselves.

Let's say you were born through happenstance, which conforms to the materialistic view of the universe where everything is created by chance. Do you know what the odds are of life forming on the third planet from the Sun, or what the odds are of Earth being at the exact distance from the Sun to allow life to form? Any closer and the Earth would be too hot and any further, Earth would be too cold. Science has never been able to replicate the exact conditions whereby the basic building blocks of life could come into being. The odds of both are actually incalculable. Winning Power ball is a sure bet in comparison. Even if the Universe, Earth and you were created by chance, then why give a shit about anything. There is a spark within you that whispers this is not so. We would all be hedonists and life's only value would be survival.

The Horse Rode Me

You know deep within you that this does not make sense. Your life would begin as nothing more than the luck of the draw. That sperm/egg combination was nothing more than chance. How does that make you feel believing that?

Then there is God as the creator, and this is wholly based on how big you conceive God to be. I'll get to God at the end of the book. Did God assign each of us to our parents? Did they have any say in the matter regarding who they got and what condition would they arrive in? Would you be healthy or marred in some way? Did either you or your parents exist before you came into your physical reality. Where does your will enter the game? Is it really free will? If you all had a vote, my guess would be that you'd vote no. So what is the purpose of this God scenario? Are you here to obey the rules you 'believe' God set forth? Are you caste down into physical form by God to learn how to rise up? Is Earth a stepping stone, and if so, a stepping stone to what? So many questions. So few answers. Maybe your understanding of God is too small.

So, getting back to the beginning of this version of you; once you squirm your way through that dark Mama tunnel and into the light of your new world you bring with you a massive puzzle that is the mosaic of your life, a swirling cacophony of beliefs and probabilities. That puzzle splinters into an untold number of pieces that you immediately begin reassembling. The first pieces you put together are the most important in setting up the intent of your life. Think of those foundational pieces of your life as the border of your puzzle. As an infant you are completely open to suggestion, particularly from your parents, but you also come with a complete set of tools you call beliefs. Everything in your reality is driven by your beliefs. Depending upon who you are born to and where you are born geographically will determine which initial tools you will activate. The beliefs you choose will be determined by your direction of exploration. You are not a 'tabula rasa', a blank slate. If you are the parent of a young child today you have probably already discovered that your child is his/her own boss. This is very different from when my father was a child and it is not because parents today are 'soft' on their kids. You are moving toward self-directing and will become more so with each succeeding generation. You could say the human race is waking up.

You are your own perfection. There is no one you need to be like, so stop trying. Just as there are no two stars exactly alike, there are no two of you. I tell you all this so that you might take back the power that is rightfully yours, the power you have abdicated to those that are prettier, stronger, smarter and more powerful. If you were meant to be like them you would have chosen differently before coming here. They are only prettier, stronger and more powerful in your own mind and based on your individual beliefs. You dealt yourself your own hand. Addicts come from all sorts of circumstances. Rich or poor, educated or uneducated, abusive or loving, your parents were your choice. Take them off your blame hook. Own your own shit, but drop the blame you caste upon yourself that might go with it. My parents were middle class, well-educated and loving, and supported me during my darkest of times. They could be annoying at times, but never did anything that someone could point to and say 'this is what drove David to the needle.' If you are religious, God does not make imperfections. You are imperfect only in your own thinking, and your thinking is not who you are. Your distorted thinking is what makes you feel like shit. It loves to compare you to others. Tell it to fuck off. My dad used to tell me that, and he was right. I didn't do it often enough, nor did I even think of doing it often enough. I always thought the Monkey Mind was telling me the truth.

You come into this reality forgetting who you are. It's part of the deal you make before entering this difficult game you have chosen to play. That's right, it is a complex game, but a game with purpose. I wish I had known that before I injected that last shot into my vein. I would have recognized all the stressors for what they are...chattering mind bullshit. You learn it all. Think about it. One of you rages out when a car pulls out in front of you when there was no one behind you. They could have waited, Right?

The Horse Rode Me

Another person doesn't give the same situation a second thought. I got a taste of Buddhism at Mountainside Rehab in Canaan, Connecticut. They talked about the Monkey Mind that chatters incessantly in your head telling you someone else put the stones in the backpack you carry around. No! You put them there. That person that pulled out in front of you is your teacher, a partner in crime, so to speak. He did not come uninvited. He's telling you something about you in that moment, and you flipping him off and blaring your horn is telling him something about himself. He is as connected to you as your toe is to your foot. But he doesn't know it any more than you do. You're both playing baseball on a basketball court with a golf club. You have the game you are trying to play all wrong.

Why did you need to forget where you came from? Why did you need to forget your power and who you are? Think about it. If you came here to experience something, let's say all the varying forms of poverty, but you remember how rich you are, you could never experience poverty in its full expression. If you get hungry you can just reach for your American Express card. It's about expanding your awareness. The primary directive of consciousness is expansion. It detests retreat and stagnation. That is why you left the caves thousands of year ago. Expansion is why you always get a kick in the ass when you get too comfortable in your safe zone. Life will throw you a motivator, whether it be a needle that rips into your arm or a tornado that rips through your home, or a disease that tares apart your body. <u>You</u> are the life that does this. Life and the Universe itself is responsive to you because it **IS** you. Move of your own free will, or get shoved. Either way it is you doing the moving **and** the shoving. Everything and everyone else are there to accommodate you. You are going to get to the other side of the street, whether you cross it directly or turn around and circle the globe to get there.

As I said before, that one-celled spermatozoa gave me a brain that enabled me to sail through school. I had a great memory. See or hear it once and it was locked and loaded. It was so easy for me that I barely had to try. It seemed to me that I was destined to make Gates-like money, and making money is your culture's prime directive. Make money or suffer is not the prime directive of the soul. The trouble was, I was paying attention to the rules of my culture and not to why I came here in the first place. It turns out that the point of my exploration was to experience the unusual, and not what my brain made easy for me. I was headed for a life of ease and ordinariness on the rich side of the scale. There was a part of me that I wasn't listening to that kept telling me that the ordinary was not what I came here for. I experienced the unusual nevertheless, the dark side of the unusual and all the heartache that goes with it.

Along with a brain that suited my culture perfectly, I was as inquisitive as a puppy exploring his environment for the first time. Anything new to my experience I had to explore. To me it was new and unusual...unusual being the key word in my case. Let this be a clue to the parents of a coming age. Pay attention to what draws your child in, for he or she is giving you information about what they are here for and not what you think is best for them. Expose them to as much as is possible for you to expose them to. Let them decide what excites them, for it may be nothing that you could have imagined. Remember, your child is not a blank slate. She is a fully formed consciousness that has chosen to experience this reality and to enter it through you. She is as magical as you are. You were never meant to be a warden. You were chosen to be a facilitator. As for the rest of you, and especially you addicts, find what moves you and realize it may be off the rails of culturally accepted explorations. Follow that. Realize that you are all connected to everything you see, hear, feel, smell and taste. Pay attention to what you are feeling as you read this book. Don't wait until you have left your physical body as I did. To do that you must understand that you are not the cause of another's feelings, just as the driver that pulled out into the road was not the cause of the driver he cut off going into a rage. You do your own and each other's bidding, but do not yet know it. Therefore, reject this phrase many of you have heard, "You'll never make a living doing what

The Horse Rode Me

you love. Get a real job." Taking that advice is a soul killer. It keeps you enslaved, stresses you out, creates anxiety and pushes you to do anything to escape.

I'm going to share with you an analogy my father told me. He said, "David, think of Anthony Hopkins sitting in a theater watching the movie, The Silence of the Lambs. The Anthony Hopkins watching the movie is the real Anthony Hopkins. Now think of yourself as David, but watching this conversation we are having from a different perspective. That you and the Anthony Hopkins sitting in the theater know that what they are viewing is a play, a much more real play for you. You each feel what the role player is feeling, for you are also the role player. In order for Hopkins to play Hannibal Lecter well he had to forget that he was Anthony Hopkins. He almost had to become Lecter. It's much the same way with us, David. The you that sits here listening to me is also the you that is viewing from that detached place. Going even further," he said, "Hopkins knows he has played many other roles, all of which added to the depth of him as an actor. He learned and expanded himself from each role. It is the same with us. Who we are in this moment adds to the depth, the wisdom, the compassion and the empathy of the larger us, who sits in a neutral place."

I sort of got it when my father first shared it with me, but I was 20 then, and really didn't give a shit. If he had shared it with me when I was two he might as well have shared it with a mushroom. Maybe that's why he didn't tell me when I was two. Maybe he didn't know it when I was two. What he left out was that Hannibal Lecter had a script. None of us have a script, but rather a general direction we want to explore. Our script is a set of probabilities from which we choose that we set before us in each moment. I should tell you that all this information is available to me now, as it eventually will be to you. It blew my mind at first, especially because my father had touched upon it when I was still alive in physical form. Not only do I know it now, I know that it has been available to all of you before there was writing. That you are connected to everything existed in stories told and retold through the generations. It has also found its way into all religions. My favorite, because of its beauty, is the Hindu metaphor of the God Indra's Net of Gems. I was actually exposed to it during my short stint at Providence College, in Providence Rhode Island. In short, Indra's Net symbolizes the Universe as a web of connections, while simultaneously emphasizing the independence of all things. The God Indra has woven a net of such immensity that it is immeasurable. It has no beginning and no end and as such it is infinite. There is a jewel at each node of the net and is arranged in such a way that each jewel reflects all others. In this way no jewel is independent of the rest. If you trust anything from the first few pages of my book, trust this. You are not alone and never have been. You do not exist because of chance or accident. That belief is a soul killer. You exist in the form that is reading this book because you chose to. Believing this is where you begin to change a fearful and stagnant system that denigrates and fears change, that believes that health, food, shelter and even love must be earned. No! You were born **AS** those things.

The Horse Rode Me

Love Is Far Bigger Than You Believe It to Be...And Far Different

My greatest challenge was learning to love myself after so many years of addiction and the darkness I swam in. I could not meet that challenge as I know many addicts cannot. You've all heard of unconditional love. So did I. I thought it was a ridiculous idea, particularly if I was supposed to feel it for complete strangers, let alone myself. After all, how can I love someone I don't know. How could I love myself unconditionally after and the pain I had caused others. Affection is born out of familiarity. I reserved my love for family and friends and pets, much as you do. I had many friends and was never without one or more pets at any one time throughout my twenty-nine years. How could I put strangers on a par with family and friends, or even my pets? You cannot love unconditionally while you continue to understand your reality as you do currently. As long as you believe a stranger is separate from you, and that he does not participate in your life, and you define love as varying degrees of affection, then the idea of unconditional love will seem a new age pipe dream.

Stories of near-death experiences all speak of feeling unconditional love. It was a feeling none of them had experienced before. They had no other words in their vocabulary to describe a feeling they never had before. The closest they could come was to add unconditional to the word love. While alive I knew my parents, Bill and Sarah and siblings, Tyler, Kailyn and Jessie, loved me. I knew the love of my life, Becky, loved me. I knew my dog Barrett loved me. It was a feeling of deep affection and connection. But, I was an addict. I couldn't believe anyone could love me unconditionally, particularly if they knew my addiction history. Parents feel it, but I was not a parent. They had to have a caveat, especially if they knew what I had done during the height of my addiction. I loathed myself. There was much in me, I thought, not to love. If you're active or recovered, you know what I'm talking about. It's the dark shit you do when you're dope sick and looking for a fix. You come to feel that no one could love such a person as that. They must be faking it, right? If you believe Hannibal Lecter is the real Anthony Hopkins, then yes, you and I were right. The reality however, is that the you that reflects back to you from a mirror is <u>the big you</u> playing a role. You have identified with the role and not the bigger you playing the role. Everyone else is doing the same damn thing. The greatest acid trip you ever had cannot shine a light on the trip you're having right now.

In Anita Morjani's book, Dying To Be Me, what she describes as unconditional love in her near death experience is total unconditional acceptance. It was so foreign to what she felt for and from her husband, her parents, her friends. It was so overwhelming that she wanted to stay within its embrace forever. It was the feeling of complete non-judgment. What she felt was the feeling I felt when I first left my body and continue to feel now. The difference is that I know what it is, maybe because I did not return as Anita Morjani did. Mine was a full death. Not a near death. It is not unconditional love. It is unconditional Acceptance without judgment. What is it that generates that kind of acceptance? It is every single soul that sits in that neutral place watching that aspect of itself playing a role. It is particularly important for those that continue in the darkness of addiction to understand this. You have never been alone. In the deepest sense, even your enemies are an intimate part and in total collusion with the exploration you have chosen, as difficult as it seems. I know it sounds crazy to you, but that craziness is based wholly upon what you believe about your

The Horse Rode Me

life, even life itself in the larger sense.

I remember how different I felt when I was in a place surrounded by close friends compared, say, to a similar situation surrounded by complete strangers. You remember it, too. You're relaxed. You're comfortable, you're at peace, or at least as much at peace as you can be with the current beliefs you hold. Now, think what it would be like if you felt the same peace in the room filled with strangers as you do in a room filled by your best friends. Multiply that by the number of stars in the sky. That is how I feel now and how you could feel now. I can tell you it is an infinitely better feeling than the first high you got from shooting up. In fact, the effect you get from heroin is pitiful compared to what is right within your reach...total and unconditional acceptance of who you are. But acceptance in and of itself is not love. You do not have to love what you accept, but you do have to refrain from judgment. You can practice by seeing everything in front of you as the cast and props in a movie you are starring in. It is all responsive to you as you are responsive to them. You are the star in your movie and a cast member in theirs, and yet you are all ONE.

The deepest and most universal form of Love is comprised of two parts. The first is <u>Knowing.</u> It is knowing that you and everything in your world is literally connected by that beautiful Web of Gems, and all of it is in partnership with you and everything else. It is an intricately choreographed dance of unimaginable complexity that is written and rewritten in each and every moment. You attract what you believe, and all of your world knows what it is you believe in each and every moment. It will faithfully reflect it back to you in a movement of great love. One of the many horrors of addiction is that your beliefs that created it snowball into an avalanche of negative beliefs about you and the world you live in. The world of connections, neutral in nature and in loving response, gives you exactly what you believe, exactly what you are focused on. It <u>Never</u> judges the beliefs. This is the acceptance I spoke of earlier. Anthony Hopkins, sitting in the theater, never judged Clarice for he knows she is playing her role perfectly. Jodi Foster, sitting in the theater, in similar fashion did not judge Hannibal Lecter.

"I wish I knew then what I know now." We've all said it. You gain some bit of knowledge along the way that you could have applied effectively to an earlier you. When I arrived on the "other side" that was exactly what I said. It was a major What The Fuck! At the same time, however, I felt no remorse, even towards those I hurt, and no blame for those that hurt me. I understood that they too were Anthony Hopkins sitting in their own theater. You are all drawn to the energy you project and that energy is belief driven. Knowing this, I mean really knowing it, has the power of creating a whole new world, where hurting another would anathema and equivalent to cutting off your own arm. It would be a world where you no longer have to throw your body on the point of a sharp needle. This is the Knowing part of love. It is not necessary to include affection, although affection often accompanies Knowing.

<u>Appreciation</u> is the second part. You understand the word in its smallest form. You appreciate someone for holding the door open for you. You appreciate a driver putting on her directional signal. You appreciate the scent of a flower. Simple things. Rarely do you appreciate stepping in dog shit...probably never. Rejection by another is not appreciated, except possibly in retrospect when we realize that the rejection eventually led to finding the love of your life. The appreciation I am speaking of includes the good, the bad and the ugly. You have chosen a playground where one of its many components is <u>duality</u>. It is duality that allows you to experience yourself as an individual. You know you are short because of those that are tall. You know you are skinny because of those that are fat. You know you are strong because of those that are weak. Without duality there would be no choice, no preferences. You know hot because there is also cold. If you are beautiful you should bless the ugly every day of your life, for without them you would not feel so appreciative of your beauty. In fact, you would not know you are beautiful.

The Horse Rode Me

A problem in your reality is that you only appreciate the good. It makes sense considering how little you understand the reality you have chosen. Keep in mind, you are not the role you are playing. You are the viewer of the role player and everything is in cahoots with you and your role. Everything knows their role perfectly and never screws it up. Before you came here you agreed to this format. The play, however is not set. It is free-form and based on probabilities you set before yourself in each moment. As I said, there is no script. You are never a victim. Every moment is an agreed upon choice between you and the dance partner you have invited to share the present moment's dance. Your partner can be a person, place or thing. It doesn't matter. It could be the chair upon which you stub your toe. You have invited it to you and it has invited you to it. It is a magnetic-like energy attraction whereby you are showing yourself, by way of reflection, something about yourself in that moment. The appreciation is of yourself for participating in their dance as much as it is an appreciation of them participating in yours. So, this deepest form of love is knowing that everything is literally connected and as such reflects aspects of yourself as much as you reflect to them, and appreciating your own and everyone else's willingness to participate in such a complex and difficult reality. Coming here, depending on what you have chosen to explore, can be a most brave endeavor. Your moment to moment surroundings are your best mirror of your inner state of being in that moment.

The Horse Rode Me

The Horse Rode Me

Beautiful Boy

Affection is a different thing. It has many degrees of intensity and varying levels of acceptance. It does not include knowing and appreciation as I described it above. While still residing within my skin I read that Eskimos have as many words for snow as there are forms of snow. Your English language has one word for love. So, when you speak of unconditional love the application of it becomes confusing. The closest you come to it is the love of a parent for their child. Through all the horror I put my parents through, they continued to love me. Don't get me wrong. We had some horrific fights. I remember leaving the house one day with a gym bag full of my Mother's family silver. Yes, they were both home and my father came out and grabbed the bag from me. I was pissed that he didn't trust me. Can you imagine? I'd already pawned his Ipad and some tools as well as other pieces of jewelry. Why in the world would he think I had anything other than gym clothes in the gym bag? Could it be because I didn't belong to a gym at the time? Could it be my altered personality? Could it be my glassy eyes or maybe it was because I had been on a several year high streak? Despite his anger he still held me tight in his heart as did my mother, but they wound up with the gym bag and silver. I wound up at Mohegan Sun Casino and OD'd in a bathroom stall. My father got the call and stayed with me in the hospital emergency room until I was given the all clear to go home. That intense level of affection is the hardest to break. And that level of horror, the hardest to accept.

The Horse Rode Me

My parents referred to me as their Beautiful Boy, a term they first learned after reading David Sheff's book, Beautiful Boy. They sent me off to my first Rehab with Sheff's book in tow, hoping to get their Beautiful Boy back. My sobriety lasted a week. My parents loved me through it all by keeping their focus on their Beautiful Boy, who was slowly encasing himself in shit. It's a little like seeing Anthony Hopkins in the audience and ignoring Hannibal Lecter on the screen. That inner light that shined so brightly for them before I started using was slowly being extinguished by me. That's right. That's what heroin does. It puts out the fire that is the light. My parents would gladly suffer the most horrendous death if their suffering could guarantee my total release from the Horse that was riding me. I remember vividly, in my current state of understanding and peace, my mother running out of the house to confront my dealer who had driven up our hill to make a delivery. She was in a rage. "If I ever see you again," she screamed, "I will find a way to take you out." He had a gun on his front seat. There was something he saw in her that convinced him of the truth in her words. He put his car in reverse, turned around and drove back down the hill. He never came to my house again, but he did come...again and again. What they dealt with at home was a Sunday school picnic compared to what they never knew, because I could never tell them.

From what I can tell from my current perspective, a mother's love for her child is the strongest on the planet under your current understanding of what love is. I didn't understand that while alive, only other mothers understand it. I was truly my mother's Beautiful Boy. In a world where you all feel separate the process of pregnancy and birth is THE closest any of you feel to full connection. That deep feeling of connection can also appear in the heat of battle where a soldier is willing to put his life at risk for his comrades. You have plenty of posthumous Medal of Honor recipients to prove the point. These are rare instances of that inner knowing arising during moments of extreme stress. Not knowing who you are nor what the rules of your reality are keeps you from enjoying the overwhelming support available to you in every moment of your life. Everything you perceive is connected to you by that Net of Gems.

I loved Philly steak sandwiches. I loved hot showers. I loved music...at least music that excited me. No. That was not love. If anything is was a watered-down version of appreciation, defined as "the recognition and enjoyment of the good qualities of someone or some thing." Even love is defined as a deep feeling of affection, and most often includes appreciation, but not the appreciation I described earlier. You will not experience unconditional love for yourself or for anything else while operating under these old definitions of these words. This topic is critically important for all of you and in particular everyone involved in the heroin epidemic. Here's why.

The Horse Rode Me

The Symbolism of the Heroin Epidemic

Recall that I stated that one degree of separation between an individual and knowing someone touched by heroin is an epidemic and that the epidemic is a symbol. I followed that with a description of Acceptance, Knowing and Appreciation. The short version of what the heroin epidemic represents is a deep sense of individual disconnect from the culture as currently constituted. In one way or another you all feel disconnected, but addicts feel it the most deeply and are your symbols of it. In your attempt to experience that deep connection by shooting up, you actually deepen the disconnect. By way of explanation I will use myself as an example. I would have been thirty years old in December 2017, well on my way to the "American Dream" had I not fallen under the spell of heroin. The dream itself is not false. What IS false is what you are told you need to do to get to it, whatever IT is. Typically, it is defined as the acquisition of the "finer" things of life. For most of you it is forty-plus hours a week of toil keeping your "nose to the grindstone" and you just might be able to afford a shiny new car, a home to live in, food to eat, life insurance...the list goes on. It is a Faustian bargain...costume jewelry in exchange for your soul. This can never work for all as long as you continue to believe you are not connected to each other.

Like you, I was fooled, but it was me fooling myself. You were

The Horse Rode Me

taught to be rational and if you were "lucky" as I was you may have been exposed to things that expand your soul rather than things that teach you to fit in. That exposure was not what you call luck. In choosing my parents the probabilities were that I'd be exposed to such things...middle class things...American things. My father is a life long distance runner and a thinker. My mother is as eclectic as a quilt woven from random pieces of cloth. I was playing soccer and T-Ball at three, learning the guitar at five and reading Stephen King at eight. There was no talk about being a doctor or a lawyer or a financial adviser. That was baked into the belief systems of the culture and I was an avid consumer of all media forms. It was my mother that exposed me to music...The Doors, Hendricks, Clapton, Santana, Led Zeppelin and the Stones were some of her favorites. There was a soft voice in my head that would whisper "follow me" whenever I would lose myself in my music. But, there was a louder voice, a scream almost, that countered the soft voice with, "you'll never make any money doing what you love. You'll never be a Hendrix. Follow the money." You have all heard that loud irritating voice, but so have you heard that soft whisper. The loud voice comes from your Western Civilization and is the voice of the Monkey Mind. That out-of-control simian loves to fit in. The soft whisper is YOU.

If I knew then what I now know I would have listened to that soft voice. I would have known, without doubt, that the entire Universe was there to support me. Why? Because the Universe IS me. It is as much a part of me, and you, as the heart is a part of the body. It is as much as part of you as Hannibal Lecter is a part of Anthony Hopkins. You are separated from nothing, connected to everything. You believe you are a separate hunk of flesh and bone that came together randomly. And why shouldn't you believe that. After all it was drilled into your head from the first time you peed in your diaper. It is a culturally induced belief, as most beliefs are. Sure, my parents planned on having me, but they also believed that who they got was random. Would I be a girl? Would I be a boy? Would I be tall like my mother or short like my father? Would I have the blue eyes of my mother or the brown eyes of my father. It

The Horse Rode Me

was all a roll of the dice to them. NO, IT WAS NOT! I chose everything about ME. They merely agreed to have me. If you are a parent, think how different you would feel if you knew that your child actually chose you over billions of others and that you agreed to her choosing.

It is so Important that you all believe this. Listen to the whispering voice. It would change everything. Planned pregnancies or unplanned pregnancies are agreements and the physical form of the child is the child's choice. To those of you that may have chosen physical disabilities and or abusive parents, and scream out to whatever God you scream to, "Woe is me. I didn't choose to be here," I say this to you. There is great purpose to your choice and it has nothing to do with suffering, even though when you made the choice there was a high probability that you would suffer because of what you would eventually believe about yourself and your reality. There is no nobility in suffering. Within your current system of beliefs, you learn to suffer. You've heard this before and probably thought it was bullshit as I did. The only value of suffering is its potential to teach you how not to suffer. You will never believe that until you believe what I am telling you in this book.

Before heroin found its way into the lives of everyone, rich and poor and everything in between, little attention was given to addiction. Why? Because those of you who control the purse strings felt no connection to the poor of the inner cities, and the rest of you were sound asleep. Heroin addiction was treated as a crime of the poor and the black, worthy of imprisonment, but surely not compassion. When the addiction of the poor and the blacks didn't move you to compassion and empathy the web of Gems widened its caste. The first wave of addiction soldiers failed to move you. They were black, brown and white...but mostly poor and without a voice. We were the second wave. You had reserved your compassion, when it appeared at all, for "real" problems like cancer. After all, you believe people with cancer didn't choose cancer. Addicts choose to use. Cancer is not chosen...or so you believe. You are selective with both your compassion and your empathy and it is not based on your feelings of connectedness, which you have little, but on the worthiness of the individual receiving your compassion and empathy. This is what a belief system does that says you are a random occurrence in a machine-like universe, and separate from each other. You must be worthy. You must EARN your acceptance. Indeed, you must earn your right to live. You must earn your value. I felt I must earn everything and when everything went to shit with my addiction, my self-esteem went into an outhouse hole. No one knew that, even after I got clean. How could they? I had the All American traits. From the outside I looked perfect. Not wanting to burden my friends and family, I never told them the truth.

I got physically fit, opened a Crossfit gym with my buddy, who was also a recovered addict, and outwardly I fit the accepted American profile. Inwardly I was a mess, but hopeful. We named our gym Crossfit Payback, for we both felt we had much to atone for. The darkness of heroin addiction doesn't evaporate when you stop using. Our Grand Opening was in April, 2014 and from the beginning it was a hit. I was happy. We were giving back to the community and I regularly visited Rushford Rehabilitation Center in Middletown, Connecticut where I shared my experiences with those struggling with their own recovery. I understood them and their struggles. I felt compassion and empathy for them, and really for everyone. I suppose you could say compassion and empathy was the gift of my addiction. Crossfit Payback membership was up and I was making a little money, not enough for a shiny new car, but I was getting by and I was clean. A year and a half later my box partner relapsed and everything went to shit from that point on. The largest boulder in my backpack reared its ugly head with a vengeance. Its name is Anxiety and if you are an addict you know its name well. Xanax was the drug of choice for this beast. My Monkey Mind rarely allowed me to remain in the present moment.

Anxiety is a sense that tomorrow with bring trouble, even though the sun shines brightly today. For me, the wolf of relapse was always just a bite of the Achilles behind me. Probably for you, too. After all, you all learn in rehab that relapse may occur during your recovery. What I heard was, "You will relapse." I was hyper vigilant, always wondering when it would come. Many of my friends are here with me because they relapsed. My anxiety, however was not just about relapsing. It was global. Will I be able to pay the rent? Will I be able to keep the gym functioning? What if too many members quit the gym? I was filled with "what ifs" that never came and yet drove me to my knees. Anxiety is a function of not being present in the moment. It is a function of the Monkey Mind. There are so many of you, sober or hooked, just one illness away from living on the street. One pink slip and you're done. In a world where people believe that everything ripples out and touches everything else these types of apprehensions should never occur, and yet they are common place where you believe you are separate from your neighbor and that you exist in a meritocracy that is unforgiving of your past.

Look to nature as your guide. She shows you the way in every moment. You ARE Safe, unless you're not. I'm not trying to be glib. Post that phrase on your bathroom mirror...You Are Safe. You live in a safe world unless you choose to believe you do not. Even then, if you look around your immediate surroundings you will see that you are safe. No one has a knife to your throat. A dog isn't chewing on your leg. You may be cold and hungry, but You Are Safe. You may be listening to the news that is showing another mass shooting in your schools, but You Are Safe. You will feel compassion and empathy for suffering children for you are connected to them, but YOU Are Safe. A cat does not run up a tree because it hears a dog bark three blocks away. It continues to bathe itself in the sun. Anxiety is fear that is based on **NOTHING** that is real in the moment. Practice looking around you. You may not like your surroundings, but you will notice you are safe. I did not do this enough. My entire nervous system was sparking flames. I turned to Xanax, and that was the beginning of the end. The Xanax made it easier to relapse.

The Horse Rode Me

Everyone was supportive even though I didn't understand why. I let them down. I got clean at Rushford and stayed clean for a few months. The stress was intense. I bought out my partner who was still using, and now everything was on me. Looking back on it from my current perspective I can see how much I was loved. The members of Crossfit Payback came together as a community and supported me fully. A few bailed, which was their right to do, but their leaving hurt. I might have too in their place. Long story short, I relapsed again, overdosed three or four times and then the deadly OD on April 3, 2017.

A week before my final OD I was nodding off (I don't mean dozing off) in my parents living room. My father interrupted whenever I nodded. I noticed he had a curious look on his face. He asked where I went each time I nodded off. My answer was simple. "I go to a place of peace." That peace, however, was not the same peace I find where I am now. It was more a void where nothing was connected, because there was nothing there. No bills to pay. No one to please. Nothing I had to be. Just Nothing. I felt nothing. This was so different than my death experience that it is difficult to explain. Where I am now, I feel connected to everything and a part of it at the same time. I am an eddy in an ocean of consciousness that holds no judgment whatsoever. That is real peace and nothing like the false peace heroin brings. What I am getting at is that you can experience my kind of peace without visiting me here.

The Horse Rode Me

Worry and Guilt

Worry and Guilt are learned behaviors in your world and arise from the 'shoulds" and 'should nots' that you learn and then believe from your earliest age. Why feel guilt or worry if everything and everyone is playing a role in your drama and have agreed to do so. Believing you are separate necessitates certain acceptable and non-acceptable behaviors. You all want to "fit in", but by trying to fit in you lose your uniqueness and then judge those that are different. What you bring with you into this world is a mandate to do no harm. However, you live in a world where what it is you believe is the engine that drives your experience. There is a natural form of guilt and you don't even have to think about it. It occurs when you do harm. Any other form of guilt is learned and unnatural. Natural guilt is felt and quickly disappears. Learned cultural guilt lingers and comes back time and time again. Let it go. If you are an addict it does nothing for your recovery. If you feel guilty because you are not feeling guilty, let that go, too. Keep in mind that all experience is within agreement between the parties involved in the experience. Each or all of you gets something from the experience, whether you think it's good or bad. After reading this you may be the only party that realizes it, though. You can laugh if you like.

Many of you, whether in recovery or not, probably are dealing with low self-esteem, as I was. When I was actively using, I stole when I could, always lied (especially to my parents) and just did

The Horse Rode Me

whatever I had to do to either get high or keep from getting dope sick. I broke just about every norm you have for civilized behavior. What hurt the most was what I was doing to those I loved. That was the guilt, and it lingered and festered. Relapses pumped up the guilt tenfold. You cannot be in the present moment with guilt. It always throws you into the past. So, guilt is your signal that you are no longer present. You've heard the expression before. It's called being in the NOW. It is not bullshit. Now is all you have and the Monkey Mind is what is blocking the gate to Now. Here are a few of the things the Monkey Mind will scream at you. You're a prick and a low life. If you really love those you say you do you wouldn't use. You're weak. You have no will power, and the big one...it's not my fault. The list is quite long. Guilt kills self-esteem and heroin use severely alters your personality. Your parents and non-using friends will attest to that. Trust me, you become a real asshole.

Get good with yourself. Appreciate your uniqueness...every day. Your mere existence means you fit in. If you draw to yourself someone that tweaks you, remember you have done this for a purpose, just as the person you have drawn has also drawn you for their purpose. It is a mutual dance. Remembering this will help with your feelings of guilt. The other bad guy is worry. It is the opposite of guilt in that worry takes you out of the present and throws you into the future. Worry is a mild form of fear. You worry about something that is not real for it does not exist in the present. This is not to say you should not prepare for the future. Do your prep work then let it go. Trust that it will manifest for you. Preparation is action. Worry is the Monkey Mind in action, taking you out of your only point of power, The Now. Worry also contributes and is the precursor of anxiety and fear. It is a fear of the future, a fear of the not now.

From my current perspective the Monkey Mind is in large part responsible for your current state of affairs both individually and collectively. The Monkey Mind operates out of the thinking mind, whose main function has been usurped by it. The Monkey Mind

The Horse Rode Me

thrives on pointing out differences, both good and bad, or at least what you deem to be good and bad. All prejudices are born out of the Monkey Mind, for they are learned and not innate. If you think you are not good enough it is the Monkey Mind talking. In each moment you are the perfect you. I don't care if you're sleeping in the gutter or taking a dump in a church yard. From my perspective you are and always have been perfect. Desiring to change (you probably refer to it as improving) is natural to consciousness as its primary directive is to expand. Everything you experience is directly related to this expansion. It comes to show you something about you.

You're at the checkout at the grocery store and are in a hurry. You've chosen the shortest line, but the person in front of you is an 80-year-old woman who has one item, a tube of Preparation H. You're feeling good about your choice of checkout lines. The cashier rings up $15.98 and you think how lucky you are not to have roids. That shit's expensive. The old woman reaches into her purse and pulls out a ten and two ones, So far so good. She then reaches back into her purse and pulls out a bulging change purse, slowly opens it and begins pulling out one coin at a time. They are all dimes and nickels. You begin questioning your choice of checkout lines as your impatience rises along with your blood pressure. She's counting as she places each coin on the counter...$12.10, $12.15. The woman has now become your enemy. She gets to $14.55 and stops. She loses her count, the clerk wasn't paying attention and she begins over again. You whisper an audible WTF. You look to your left and the shopper with a full cart is done checking out and the Monkey Mind begins telling you that you always chose the wrong line. The old woman appears to validate what the Monkey Mind just told you. What she is really doing is validating what it is you already believe about yourself and old people.

Do you see yourself in this scenario? Does it trigger compassion and empathy for the old woman? I doubt it. So, what was this woman, draw by you to be in front of you, trying to teach you in

The Horse Rode Me

this moment. Your emotions tell the tale. Your emotions went from impatience to frustration and finally to anger. That is what she was showing you. You blamed her for being old, for making you late for whatever you were in a hurry for, for being nothing more than a nuisance as well as validating your belief that you always choose the wrong line. You felt stuck and saw no other choices in front of you. You could have offered to count out her change for her or at the least keep count along with her so she wouldn't have to begin over. You could have left. There are always other choices. Nothing is ever either black or white. You have been taught by way of your beliefs to choose either black or white when in reality there is a rainbow in between.

At this point in my book my father went upstairs for a thirty-minute ride on his spin bike. My energy was hovering around him. I like watching him work out while he listens to his music. When Neil Young came on singing Rockin' In The Free World. I let him know that I wanted the lyrics put right here. Put the book down. Find the music. Listen to the music. Listen to the lyrics. Dance!

There's colors on the street
Red, white and blue
People shuffling their feet
People sleeping in their shoes
There's a warning sign on the road ahead
There's a lot of people saying we'd rather be dead
Don't feel like Satan, but I am to them
So I try to forget it any way I can

Keep rockin' in the free world
Keep rockin' in the free world
Keep rockin' in the free world
Keep rockin' in the free world

I see a woman in the night
With a baby in her hand
There's an old street light
Near a garbage can

The Horse Rode Me

Now she put the kid away and she's gone to get a hit
She hates her life and what she's done to it
There's one more kid that'll never go to school
Never get to fall in love, never get to be cool

Keep on rockin' in the free world
Keep on rockin' in the free world
Keep on rockin' in the free world
Keep on rockin' in the free world

We got a thousand points of light
For the homeless man
We got kinder, gentler machine gun hands
We've got department stores and toilet paper
Got Styrofoam boxes for the ozone layer
Got a man of the people says keep hope alive
Got fuel to burn, got roads to drive

Keep on rockin' in the free world
Keep on rockin' in the free world
Keep on rockin' in the free world
Keep on rockin' in the free world.

These are lyrics from a man who knows we have screwed up and got things wrong. He knows why you got angry standing behind that old lady. He knows the pain of your addiction. He knows you are not free. He too was addicted, got clean and learned and expanded from the experience.

The Horse Rode Me

If You're Not Free, What Are You?

Can you ever really be free if you don't know who you are? Are you free if you cross the street so as not to have to walk past a homeless person? Are you free if you stop at a stop sign even when no other vehicle is in sight? Are you free if you wear a suit to work when you'd rather wear jeans and a T? Are you free if you want to buy a steak, but have to settle for a hot dog or Ramen, or even worse go dumpster diving? Are you free if you'd like to approach someone at a party, but something keeps you from doing so? I say you are not, and certainly if you are using dope you are not free. You are in a high security prison. All of you are not free from worry or guilt. Very few of you appreciate anything other than what you like, and even fewer love anything other than who or what you have affection for. This is so because from the beginning of human time you have been playing a game where you have purposely forgotten not only who you are, but the rules of the game as well. You have been stuck on an endless hamster wheel, doomed to repeat the horrors of your past. The good news is that you have collectively chosen to gradually remember who you are and the rules of your physical game. Your old methods will no longer work.

You have chosen to be alive during the most significant change in human history. You are very brave for choosing so. Old structures are slowly crumbling to the point where you feel as though the world is falling apart. In a sense it is. Whole populations are displaced and on the move. Your climate is changing, causing further human displacement. Lands that were once fertile are drying up and lands that were once dry are becoming inundated with water. All of this you are collectively doing, and with a grand purpose. You might well ask why? The you that plays the role has always preferred the familiar, and the familiar breeds stagnation. The real you demands expansion. All of this upheaval is your kick in the ass. It is what you have chosen to be your motivator. You even elected a sleeping President to nudge into waking. You have created many such upheavals before, but on a vastly smaller scale. The displacement of people is all about connection, and the lack of connection is what the heroin epidemic is all about. That lack of connection is why many of you cross the street to avoid a homeless person...or a dope fiend.

During my darkest times I felt utterly alone in a world where everything is connected. I was living on the streets in abject degradation in a world full of abundance, a world where I should have excelled. While heroin addiction kept its place in the inner cities and out of the homes of the middle and upper classes little note was taken because you felt no connection to them. The symbol needed a larger audience, and so we chose, we soldiers of the symbol. There are millions of others. Some fleeing wild fires. Some moving to high ground from rising rivers. Some moving aside for lava flows. Some fleeing the destruction of their cities by wars that never end, and some hiding from ethnic cleansers. Ignore this at your own peril for the intensity of your self-created motivators will increase. Insurance companies will not save you from this level of human displacement. Acting as IF you were all connected would be a good beginning. Eventually you will KNOW you are.

Resurrecting your innate sense of compassion and empathy will also be necessary. Oddly enough my addiction did that for me. It could have gone the other way and it does and did for some addicts. That Beautiful Boy my parents saw in me as a child was reignited. I always stood up for the underdog because in a strange way I felt I was an underdog. Society didn't see me that way because I had chosen the perfect traits to fit in. I had a great sense of empathy because I saw myself in them. I didn't realize, of

The Horse Rode Me

course, that they were reflecting me. You don't understand how kindness, compassion and empathy reaches out and touches people. I didn't while alive. It was simply an aspect of myself that felt right. Had I held on to my normal consciousness after passing I would have been amazed at the number of people that appeared at my calling hours. Over five hundred people stood in a line that wound around the block to pay their respects. A few of them I had met only once. Their stories remain a treasure for my mother and father and I thank you all for sharing that with them. The moment I passed, however, my consciousness rejoined and thus expanded with the me, the real me, watching and feeling me play my role. And so I knew why so many came to say goodbye. They were all connected to me as much as I was connected to them. That was another WTF moment. I met Chris O'Connor when he passed and I have to say I laughed my ghost-like ass off. I knew exactly what he would say when he realized it was all a game with purpose. "WTF" he said, and we both laughed hysterically as we did when we were both alive, so to speak. Chris originated the Dopey podcast and was influential in helping an uncounted number of addicts. You could say he was the head of the spear, a brave and courageous soul. He was there to say good bye to me and I was there to greet him when he passed over. His time on earth touched many.

The Horse Rode Me

The Myths of Perfection

You strive for the good and try to avoid the bad. Many believe you do this for religious reasons or that religion keeps you from 'sinning', as if sinning was your primary cause for being where you are. You come pre-wired knowing you are connected and so harming another is the same as harming yourself. You don't need religion to feel this in your bones. It is a part of who you are. If you believe God does not create imperfections then what need is there to strive for perfection? The need comes from beliefs you have incorporated as truth. You are the complete you in every moment of your existence. You have not come into your reality tainted with sin. There is nothing you have to atone for. There is no karma. There are no endless rounds of reincarnational lives where you strive to reach perfection. There is only Now. All the rest are beliefs. You figure this out pretty quickly when you get to where I am. This knowing is what generated the WTF from Chris and I when we arrived here.

If your sense of compassion and empathy is intact enough so that you are beginning to feel a connection to everything then you will not long for the "Good Old Days." Those days were rife with exclusion, not inclusion. Rife with hierarchies. Rife with knowing your place. Rife with acceptance of the status quo. Rife with keeping people 'less' than you in their place. The good old days were when you believed white was better than black and acted on it. The good old days were when you believed homosexuality was

The Horse Rode Me

an abomination and acted on it. The good old days were when you believed women were less than men and acted on it. In the good old days you believed some people deserved a better life than others. Where do you see the good old days fitting into your ideas of perfection...perfection for who? The good old days were when you could lock up heroin addicts and forget about them. Out of sight, out of mind? But, now that they are your sons and daughters it's a different story...isn't it.

Believing you are less than who you are in any given moment needs to be untaught and must begin at birth before it becomes a rock-solid belief. Currently there is not a person on planet earth that doesn't want to change something about themselves they don't like. You are mandated to change and to expand. You are not mandated to judge what you don't like about yourself or others. There is no fate and there is no destiny. There is only choice and change. Keep in mind that acceptance does not mean you have to love or even like what it is you have accepted. You can say that you don't like something about yourself in any given moment and still be accepting without judgment. If you are overweight, accept it. If you like being overweight then no action need be taken. If you don't like being overweight then take action. You are at play in a reality of physical action. What you believe, however, is critical to manifesting what it is you want.

I had many beliefs swirling around my addiction. I believed I had to hit rock bottom before I would get help. The trouble with this belief is that the bottom kept moving lower. There is no universal rock-bottom. I believed I could not flush the poison out of my body without great suffering. Going cold turkey was out of the question. By way of comparison, I had a boil on my rectum surgically removed with nothing more than Tylenol. This was after I got clean. So, it wasn't simply fear of being uncomfortable. I had tried going cold turkey before...once. I would rather have a boil removed from my ass once a week for eternity than go through heroin withdrawal. I believed I had brain cell receptors that doomed me to a difficult recovery and addicted me in the first place. I believed that being labeled an addict precluded me from living any kind of meaningful life after recovery. I believed the world outside of addiction would not provide me with a meaningful job if they knew I was a recovered addict. Opening a Crossfit gym seemed the 'perfect' answer for me.

Perfection is a belief. It only exists in your mind. You all have differing ideals or models that you aspire to or admire in others. You also go to that place where you compare yourself to the ideal and fail in the comparison. When you look upon someone who falls lower than you in your idea of perfection, you rise in your comparison. Rarely do you think that everyone and everything is perfect as is in the moment...and that is where you trip up. You have meticulously crafted your own image. No one else has crafted that image. If you don't like it change it, but don't go blaming someone else when it was you that chose your time of entry into the world as well as your gender and your physical attributes. You chose where you would be born by way of choosing your Mother. You literally chose all the 'perfect' influences to aid you in your exploration. Those influences can be either negative or positive by your way of thinking, but are neutral from the point where you chose. The rest has always been up to you.

Like most of you I too compared myself to others before and after I became addicted. I did not, however, have a 'perfect' ideal of myself. There were aspects of others I admired and those that I did not. I stood up pretty well to those comparisons until I started using. Failing to measure up to non-users I began comparing myself to users. In my mind I was never as 'bad' as them. Even hitting rock-bottom, which my parents felt I reached many times, I knew many others that went far lower. I was miserable, hovering on the border of degradation, but so many more were more miserable. All I had was my false community of fellow addicts. They could relate. We resided in a house of cards so unstable that the slightest breeze would knock it down. Remember the Net of Gems. The entire planet is a single organism of conscious energy. You can only see yourself in relation to something else, but stop judging yourself as better or worse than.

Influences

No one can choose for you, but you can choose consciously or unconsciously to be influenced by both individuals and the society into which you chose to be born. It is that influence that establishes your belief systems. If you allow me to influence your beliefs regarding how and why you wound up here, which were the 'perfect' initial choices made by you, then you may begin to let everyone including yourself off your blame hook. You may also

The Horse Rode Me

find that you can no longer see yourself as a victim...of anything. Imagine a world where there are no victims, but rather a swirling universe of influences to choose from. You are a child in a candy store. A world with no victims is also a world where there is no one and no thing to blame. Let's consider my first choice and what it involved.

You all existed before you came into your reality, but you existed as the larger self (the Anthony Hopkins watching the movie). Let's call the larger me Split Jeans (he) and the me that my family and friends know I'll refer to as David (I). Split Jeans had a goal, just as you did. There is no separation between Split Jeans and I, but for ease of understanding I've given them separate pronouns. In the deepest sense they (Split Jeans and I) are one and the same. Think of Split Jeans as soul, or the entirety of me. You are all infinitely larger than you have been led to believe. Split Jeans had an agenda and many realities to choose from. He chose your reality because it best suited his purpose. Split Jeans has been around the block, having spent countless lives in your dimension and others. Many of those lives he shared with other souls and developed what you might call affection for them. Maybe affinity would be a better word. He enjoys exploring with them, so when he chooses, he keeps them in mind first and if they fit his intent he will choose them first. His intent was to explore and experience the unusual and knew that the moment I entered your world that I would forget that Split Jeans is me and forget what my intent was. Therefore, in choosing He/I had to consider all probabilities of how my choices might unfold. Keep in mind that some of his 'friends' will play a positive role, while others will play a negative role.

I want to back up a little before going forward with this. Time does not exist in the place where Split Jeans makes his decision. In fact, Time only exists in physical dimensions such as yours. This is why in your dreams you can dart from one time and or one place instantly. Dreams are as real as your waking, everyday reality. I'll have more on time later. In your world my parents, Bill and Sarah, already have well established belief systems that Split Jeans can see. He knows that they would be a great jumping off point into his next life exploration as me, David. He also knows the DNA structure of the exact sperm cell that best suits him. Thus, the allowance of the one sperm he has chosen to enter the specific egg Sarah has produced. Timing is important here, as Sarah produces an egg every month and so he needed just the right egg/sperm combination. You all do this before entering your world.

In addition to the right sperm/egg he needed an open culture that would provide for the probability of a broader range of choices. That Sarah and Bill lived in the US fit that bill, but that they lived in Connecticut opened even more possibilities for exploring the unusual. Connecticut was a far more open and progressive area, say, than Mississippi. That was neither good nor bad in the broadest sense. It merely fit the probability spectrum that better suited his/my intent. Obviously, Mississippi was the perfect choice for millions of other souls, all of whom had different intents. The choice of parents, location and time combined to offer the best set of probabilities for me to play with.

Once I was born, I would slowly forget that I was Split Jeans. I came into the world connected to everything and experienced it fully. I was my mother. I was my father. I was everything I experienced with my physical senses. Slowly, however, I was taught that I was separate from everything and began incorporating both my parent's and my culture's belief systems. My beliefs gradually became the film that fed my perception. Perception was the projector that played the film. What I projected outwardly became not only my reality, but my feedback system as well. It showed me what I believed and what I felt in each and every moment. Of course, I didn't know that as David. As David I forgot that I was Split Jeans. I also forgot that everything I experienced was my own projection. The most destructive and the earliest belief I learned was that I was separate from everything else. The longer I believed in my separateness the more solid the belief became. It morphed into a truth. But I wasn't left swinging from a

The Horse Rode Me

rope in a stiff breeze. I was given tools to use in navigating your world, but I didn't know I had them.

Tools of Navigation

The Body
Your **body** is so much more than the carrier of your senses. Left to its own devices it will easily ward off diseases and remain in good health. In your reality, however, it is intimately linked to your consciousness and in particular, your beliefs. It can also be one of your greatest motivators. Many of you create diseases that will move you away from a self-limiting belief. The illness can often be symbolic in its manifestation. My father exhibited a wonderful manifestation of a symbolic illness. His first kidney stone occurred shortly before I was born in 1987 and shortly after his own personal metamorphosis that ultimately allowed him to connect with my energy while writing this book. While coping with occasional kidney stones he also had severe seasonal allergies to pollen and year-round allergies to many of our animals.

He cured his allergies by realizing that it didn't make sense that he or anyone should be allergic to anything that naturally came forth from the earth, and thus created by his own perception. He felt strongly at that time that he was OF the earth. He was also in the early stages of understanding who he was, just as I understood it after my final OD. One day he walked into the woods, hugged a few trees, came back to the house and hugged our cats and dog. His allergies disappeared from that day forward. His Kidney stones took a bit longer to figure out. He eventually decided that the stones were similar to giving birth. Once he settled on the symbolism, he then had to figure what he was not giving birth to in his life. He had just started writing his first book, Gideon McGee's Dream, during one of our vacations on Topsail Island, North Carolina. It came to him while writing on the beach that it was his own creative nature that was aching to be born. In January of 1995 he sent his manuscript to the printers. Two months later on his

The Horse Rode Me

birthday he had another stone, which he needed surgery to remove. He returned home the same day, and there, sitting on his doorstep, were a thousand copies of his first book, Gideon McGee's Dream. He never had another stone.

You might say that was nothing more than a coincidence. You would be wrong. It was information that he was right about his kidney stones. Coincidences are messages from you to you. My father told me of the following coincidence of his many times when I was old enough to understand it. His story never failed to blow my mind. In 1990 he began participating in the mythopoetic branch of the men's movement. This is the branch of the movement that beats drums and does sweat lodges and was ridiculed by the network sitcoms. A sweat lodge ceremony is a Native American spiritual tradition whereby consciousness is altered through extreme heat. When I was thirteen I participated in such a ceremony with my father and three of his friends, Tom Lee, Dean Festa and Steve Hancock. Anyway, he had participated in several sweat lodge ceremonies and wanted to construct a lodge on our property. We lived atop a wooded hill and he wanted his sweat lodge below the level of the ground. At that time he was beginning to see the earth less as an accident and more as a mother, but not yet as an outer projection of himself. H still didn't see it as his own construction. He reasoned there was <u>virtually</u> nothing on the earth that didn't come out of it, so metaphorically it acted similar to a mother. And so he began digging. For those of you that know the New England woods, you know that digging a twelve yard diameter hole three feet deep is a chore more for a back hoe than a small sized man. The project took weeks, and as he neared the bottom of his dig, a large boulder began to surface. It was irregular in shape, gold in colour and had the appearance of marble. All in all a beautiful stone, but at nearly 200 pounds he knew he would need a digging bar to pry it loose. A digging bar is a heavy steel bar five feet long with a flattened, somewhat pointed end for punching holes in the earth or prying large stones out of it.

During this process he questioned whether he should be

The Horse Rode Me

changing a Native American tradition for his own purposes, and whether he should be using their tradition at all. He asked for a sign and continued to dig around the megalith that stood dead center of the lodge. His shovel hit something hard and he feared another large stone. He probed the earth with his shovel like a soldier probing for land mines. He had asked for an answer and it was given to him. He unearthed a two hundred-year-old digging bar lying next to the two-hundred-pound stone that stood dead center in his three-foot-deep and twelve feet wide sweat lodge hole. Some things are just too meaningful to be a mere coincidence, but your mesmerized worldview makes it difficult to admit publicly that deep down you really believe there is meaning in such events and that they are not accidental. They are messages that reality is more complex than you believe it to be, and once you begin believing that, 'coincidences' appear regularly.

Let's go back to that boil on my ass and the surgery it required. It was actually an anal cyst. I had a previous one removed when I was an infant. From my current perspective my body was signaling me from a very early age. As a result of my addiction I also contracted Hepatitis C from shared needles. Hep C destroys the liver, which filters and detoxifies blood coming from the digestive tract. Your current beliefs posit that I simply contracted the disease and that the cyst was formed by infection and or clogging of a gland. A purely materialistic view of the body that completely excludes consciousness. The reality is that the body reflects your beliefs and also acts as a motivator. Let's look at just these two problems in a symbolic light. The anus is the channel through which you eliminate waste products the body does not need for nourishment. The liver detoxifies and purifies blood. Both deal with waste products. I was holding on to a faulty belief that was damaging me. I needed to expel it from my belief systems. That belief was the belief in separation, that I was alone and on my own. It was a toxic belief, one held by nearly all addicts and much of the general population. Keep in mind that I didn't know all of this while still breathing the same air that you breathe.

The Horse Rode Me

People are beginning to awaken to the power of consciousness. The mind body connection is far stronger than you currently believe. In fact, the body is a manifestation of consciousness and as such is perfectly attuned to it. It responds not to what you think, but rather to what you believe. The power of positive thinking will only go so far if you have a strong belief that goes counter to it. Positive thinking regarding overcoming your addiction will run into a wall by way of your strong belief in the power of the addiction. You have the power by way of what you believe. If the symbolism of addiction is a deep feeling of disconnect, let me assure you that using dope only strengthens the feeling that you so much want to escape. Before my last relapse I was deeply stressed, filled with anxiety and felt totally alone, despite having many people that loved me. For the brief amount of time that heroin relieved those feelings with its false promise, the aftermath of the high was a significantly lower low. For change to occur in both the use and treatment of addiction you must change your current beliefs about who you are and what your reality is actually about. Treatment must include consciousness and the exploration of limiting beliefs.

The Horse Rode Me

Your Emotions

The second and greatest tool you have in navigating your world are your **Emotions**. While alive in the flesh I understood emotions to be reactions, either to external stimuli or internal memories. So do you. We both learned this from our earliest age. There was a cause that created an effect, the effect being the emotion. You call me an asshole and I feel an emotion. When I'd remember how I hurt my parents the memory causes sadness and self-deprecation. Not now, of course, but while I was still breathing your air I did. Your girlfriend breaks up with you and you feel sadness and maybe anger, or maybe even relief. It depends on the relationship you had. Let me say, however, that evoking memories from the past takes you out of the present moment and is most often the work of the Monkey Mind. <u>A lingering emotion, whether it be sadness or grief, tells you that you are not present.</u> Emotions as communications that are generated in the now moment are brief. Your reality is an exquisite mosaic of feedback loops. You are never left in the dark. But as I said before, you have morphed your beliefs to such a degree that you are trying to play baseball on a basketball court with a golf club. You are all jacked around.

You are the cause of everything you experience. Everyone and everything on the planet provide the reflection of you. How could it be otherwise if everything is connected. Your emotions tell you

The Horse Rode Me

what your inner state of mind is in that very moment you experience whatever it is you experience. If you are feeling fear in the moment, look around you. Is it real in your present experience? Probably not. If your fear is based on differences, as in fearing culturally different people migrating into your country, is it really fear or is it triggered by your dislike of people who are different? While you are reading this is there a brown skinned person holding a knife to your throat? Trust me when I tell you that they are not different than you in any way. They are in the world to reflect your own prejudices, and you theirs. They are showing you something about you. You should thank them for that, and then change what it is in you that you dislike. Do you feel different depending on the color of the person that robs you? If that person is white do you clump all whites into the category of robbers? Is it a trait of white people? If your answer is no, then it should hold no matter what race robs you. You fear what you do not understand. You are prone to scapegoating, as you think it absolves you. It does not.

Think of your feelings (sad, mad, glad, etc.) as a signal, similar to the phone ringing. The ring of the phone tells you that someone has something to say. If they are on your contact list you know before answering who is calling. You can choose to answer or not. Generally, if you don't know who is calling you don't answer the phone. With emotions it is you calling you. If you ignore what they are trying to tell you they will keep calling...over...and over...and over; first with a little tack hammer and eventually with the sledge. Your feelings are not about someone else. They are about you, and for the person you are interacting with it is about them. Not knowing this causes you great distress because you think emotions are a reaction. You believe it is about the other person and therefore learn nothing about yourself.

After I disengaged from my body some of the most beloved people in my life used the expression "Damn it, Dave," or would lovingly call me an Asshole because of the way I left. They were grieving and missed no longer having me in their lives. They also believed that my life was cut short. Trust me when I tell you it was not cut short. Regarding the emotions they felt, there are two types of emotions, those that linger and those that are brief. Grief that appears regularly and then lingers is triggered by your thinking, as lingering grief resides the past. You remember a time you had spent with me and you experience sadness, but you could also choose to experience joy. Memories carry both. When an emotion lingers you are not experiencing the present. You are reliving the past or mourning a future without me through your thinking. Snap out of it, unless, of course, you like the feeling. My guess is that you do not. <u>There is a big difference between grieving for my loss of a future and grieving for your loss of me.</u> My father understands this. When he grieves, he grieves for his loss as he knows that I, David/Split Jeans, has lost nothing. You might wonder if I grieve the loss of those I love. Let me say this. I Know and Appreciate all of you and continue to hold great fondness and affinity for those I love as defined as you currently define it. We are never separated and never have been. All of you have your own Split Jeans and that is who I am now, my full self.

Emotions are not to be judged any more than you judge the ringing of a phone. They are vehicles of alert, and as such are neutral, just as the ring of your phone is neutral. You have just presented yourself some information about you. Pick up the phone and determine what it is. The feeling, as I said, is neutral although you attach good and bad to the numerous feelings you generate. Who likes rage? I sure didn't. Rage fell in my bad box along with hate, frustration, anger and jealousy. I filled my good box with happy, joy, peace and appreciation. In and of themselves they are merely signals. The message is not the signal. The message lies within the experience you generated to create the signal and they both arise simultaneously. You're attracted to "bad boys", who are also attracted to you. At first things are great until he starts to treat you like you're a stink bug. You kick him out and wonder why you always get the losers. You get the losers because there is a part of you that believes <u>you</u> are a loser. They are reflections. Change the beliefs you have about you and what you draw to you will change in response. However, if you believe all men are losers you will give yourself ample proof.

What do you do when you believe someone or some thing is the cause of how you feel? You give away your power. "He did this to me." "She did this to me." "It did this to me." "God is punishing me." "It's karma." STOP! No one and no thing is the cause of you. You are the star of your show. When you believe someone else is the cause of your emotions you learn nothing about you. You move into blame and repeat the same patterns over and over. Self-pity is a seriously stuck place to be. So is self-deprecation.

How are those beliefs working out for you? You're told God works in mysterious ways. No! God does not work in mysterious ways. You have taught yourselves to believe in self destructive beliefs. If you are religious you are not a prisoner of God's will. If you are an atheist you are not a prisoner of blind materialism. Let your body and your emotions be your guide. They are your greatest communicators.

Impulses

Your third tool of navigation is your <u>impulses</u>. I didn't have any religious training even though my parents had me Baptized in the Episcopal Church. Their thinking was that should I ever feel a need to turn to a religion it might be helpful if I was already baptized. I suppose you could say I turned to heroin instead. The reason I bring up religion is because historically they have tried to repress your human impulses, believing they are driven by your impure "animal nature," which they believed to be evil. This belief has been a disaster for the human race. It's like forbidding a bloodhound from using its nose. It has grown so ridiculous that some fringe groups believe that masturbation is akin to killing a potential baby. If this was so the combined deaths of all your wars for all time would pale in comparison. Your impulses have, from the beginning of your time, always been an inner guidance system. You have warped them to the point that they now appear as dark urges when and if they appear at all. Any psychologist worth the title will tell you that what you do not bring into the light of day will manifest during the darkness of night. In other words, what you repress will morph into something dark that if initially allowed its free flow would have been helpful to you. It is the classic tale of Dr. Jekyll and Mr. Hyde.

I encourage you to understand impulses as a brief in-the-moment guidance system. An example would be an urge to call a friend you haven't spoken to for some time. You make the call and discover that your friend was thinking of you just as the phone rang. The call rekindles a relationship that moves you in a new direction. Another example might be looking for a specific book and while doing so a different book jumps out at you triggering an urge to buy it. You do so and the book winds up changing your life. Here is an impulse that was critical in my life. I remember vividly having an impulse to walk away the first time I was introduced to Oxycontin. Had I followed that impulse my life would have been entirely different. Impulses will never lead you to traverse the circumference of the globe just to get you to the other side of the street. Impulses are fleeting and easy to ignore when you believe they are meaningless. By ignoring them you are moving out of the stream of your life. They are meant to keep you in your own flow, but they never force you to follow their gentle nudge. That would negate free will. It is always up to you to choose. Where did that impulse of mine come from? It came from Split Jeans, who is as much me as Anthony Hopkins is Hannibal Lecter. Your own "Split Jeans" is always available to you.

There is no such thing as an impulse to use dope, especially when it comes to relapses. You never relapse on an impulse. You agonize over the decision. Impulses are fleeting, so fast that you barely notice them. They are like a sudden gust of wind on a Summer day. They cool you off and then they're gone. They will never say, "Hey go get addicted so you can wind up in the gutter," or "go shoot someone," or "go rob a bank." You can separate a real impulse from your thinking mind by the fact that an impulse rarely repeats itself. They will never steer you in the wrong direction and the more you follow their direction the easier it will be to hear them. If you're a vegan and have an urge to have a cheese snack, go for it. The world will not collapse under you. Practice listening, but more importantly, act on your impulses. You can thank me when you get here.

Imagination
Your fourth tool is <u>imagination</u>. It is imagination that leads to inspiration. Day dreaming is not imagination. Sometimes what you imagine takes generations to appear in your reality. You might think what good does it do me if I can't experience what it is I imagined. To answer that question, I'd have to get into an explanation of time and your faulty ideas about it. I'll do that later, however. Imagining human flight and walking on the moon are two examples of imagination leading to inspiration, leading into manifestation. Keep in mind that we are all connected not only physically by way of the energy of consciousness, but also in time. I don't have to guess that you are more interested in you and in your time. I was too, when I was with you.

Imagination roams outside the box of your accepted beliefs. Picture a giant container vessel where the entire ship is stacked end to end, front to back and top to bottom with steel containers. These are your beliefs. The stronger your belief in something the more difficult it is to imagine anything outside the box of that particular belief. You have many beliefs revolving around money. They are as solid as Superman's skin and thus create a goodly amount of black and white thinking. It's difficult to imagine how the world might work without money. What would happen to your economy? What value would hard work have? Without a world dependent upon money for the basic necessities of life there would probably be no incentive to produce heroin. In fact, there would probably be no cartels to produce it. Imagine time travel. It will not happen by way of a machine, but by an expansion of consciousness. For now however, imagine a drug that will get you off heroin without addicting you to the very drug you're using to quit. When there are profits to be made from drug production, addicting you to the drug is in the best interest of the drug company making the drug. This is another reason to imagine a world independent of money. A precursor to this moneyless world is the belief everyone and everything is connected. When that belief takes hold everyone and everything would take great care to do no harm. It would be a world of cooperation and not of competition.

So how does imagination have an impact? First you must understand that consciousness does not reside within the body. The body resides within the consciousness field. In other words, the body resides within the soul. It connects with the energy of everything else. Imagination comes from consciousness, and so everything you believe and imagine touches everything else. It is therefore affecting. The more people that imagine the same thing the greater the chance what is imagined will make it into physical reality. When you believe that consciousness is manufactured and resides within the brain you severely limit yourselves. My father once shared this analogy with me. Imagine an alien ship lands next to your house and two creatures exit their ship and walk into your house. The television is on and they look curiously at it. It seems to them that the images and audio is produced from within the TV. To test their theory, they cut a wire and the sound goes off, seemingly validating their theory. They splice the wire together and the audio comes back on. They cut another wire and the picture goes out. Once spliced together the picture returns. You and I know that the audio and the picture is produced outside the set, and the set becomes impaired if tampered with. Or, you can buy a lemon TV to begin with. It is the same with our brains. Damage the brain and the physical conduction of consciousness is altered, but only within the body. Consciousness cannot be destroyed. Only the conduit for consciousness can be impaired. Remember this when interacting with those you call mentally challenged.

I tell you this so that you might alter a very limiting belief and thus expand your ability to alter your immediate circumstances. Without imagination you would all still be living in caves. It is an inherent faculty that you have ignored for far too long. You must reawaken it. Just as the body responds to Crossfit training so do the

The Horse Rode Me

tools of navigating your world improve with practice. When you believe you create all of your experience then you become the master of your own ship. It's time to get off auto pilot and take the helm. Get off the basketball court. Ditch the golf club. Walk to Yankee Stadium and on your way stop at a sporting goods store and pick up a baseball, glove and bat. It's time you all begin playing the game the way it was meant to be played.

The Horse Rode Me

The Horse Rode Me

There Is No Normal

Have you ever wondered why you're all so different? Probably not. The word 'Normal' however, suggests there is some cosmic cookie cutter into which you must fit. Normal, that most odious of words, was invented to keep you conformed to the rules of the culture you chose to be born into. You feel that you have to fit in, but you have put your world together in such a magnificently magical way so as to offer you limitless choices. You play in a reality of infinite gradations of color, sound, odors, textures, tastes...and people, places and things. Is there a normal color? Is there a normal sound? Is there a normal odor? Is there a normal taste? No there is not, although you develop preferences for each of them. So why do you believe there is a normal Human being? You are unique by your own choosing. Your favorite color may be red, but that doesn't relegate all other colors to the bowels of hell. There are other colors so that you <u>WILL</u> develop preferences. You like red. I like blue. Which one of us is right?

You choose your own unique likes and dislikes all in alignment with what you have chosen to explore. You would not develop a preference for red hair if everyone had red hair. You would not have a preference for blue eyes if everyone had blue eyes. You only like big noses because you have seen large noses and small noses. You are bombarded with images of movie stars on your media and you begin comparing. How do you measure up? How do you feel if you do and if you don't measure up? Do you begin to emulate them? Do you want to disappear if you don't even begin to measure up? Will you not accept yourself as you are now and beat yourself up until you reach that ideal? You <u>can</u> aspire to change. It is the mandate of consciousness. You play in a reality that requires action. As I said, you <u>Will</u> have preferences, likes and dislikes, and to acquire your likes demands action. You will get what you focus upon, so focus on what you like. If you focus on what you don't like then what you don't like is what you will get. You will get the self you focus on.

It is therefore critical that you focus on that which you desire and not upon that which you do not desire. This is particularly important for addicts. You always attract what you focus upon. If you focus on what you do not like about yourself then that is what you will keep. In this process try your best to eliminate your beliefs revolving around your ideas of normal and perfect. Accept without judgment your current self. I don't care how screwed up you <u>think</u> you are, it is your creation and fully worthy of your acceptance in each and every moment. You will be moved to change either by way of your conscious volition or unconscious volition. The unconscious will motivate you by way of small or large traumas. Those will be what you currently refer to as accidents or victimizations. Keep in mind, you currently see yourself as a victim of disease, along with everything else you believe you did not consciously choose. I am not referring here strictly to body type and appearance. You not only believe there are normal and abnormal body types, you believe the same about personality types.

You can have the body you desire and a personality that you hate. Addicts often feel this disparity between the outer image and the inner self. Beauty, in and of itself, can be both a blessing and a curse. In one respect a 'real beauty' can be both admired and loathed simultaneously. People may take action to mimic that beauty while simultaneously demeaning the personality of the beauty. They may be selfish, pompous and use their beauty for an advantage that the non-beauty may not have. Of course, this may be completely untrue. While still alive I found that women who I felt were a ten often saw themselves as a 5, while men who I saw as a five often felt they were a 10. This disparity was completely based on the beliefs the culture induced. Addicts, at the height of their addiction, saw themselves as a 1. Both beauty and personality is severely altered by heroin and never completely recovers because of what you believe. This is because both the addict and the general population never embraced their connection to each other, and therefore are unable to practice acceptance, let alone appreciation. When you believe you are separate then words like normal and perfect are able to gain a foothold. You are each your own normal, each your own perfection. Don't wait until you get to visit with me here to realize this.

The Horse Rode Me

Parents and Loved Ones

You cannot save anyone, let alone an addict. Even in battle one soldier cannot save another if it is not his choice to be saved. This battlefield type of saving is different than trying to save someone from themselves. In fact, in your attempts to "Fix" them you can influence them in the opposite direction of your attempts to do so. Your attempts to fix and direct are a not so subtle way of saying, "I know what is best for you far more than you do." This is an actual discounting of the choices they have made that led them to their addiction. Those choices have purpose and direction. Split Jeans never judged Me as David throughout the entirety of my life in your physical reality. He, just as your own Split Jeans, sits in a place of total acceptance; that place that Anita Morjani described in her book Dying To Be Me. This is no easy thing to do while holding to your current beliefs about what you're doing here and what you believe are the rules of your game. You so intensely identify with the role your loved one is playing, and your own, that you cannot see or even imagine the larger Self of the loved-one you are trying to save/fix. When your child suffers you naturally want to steer him or her away from their suffering. It is your sense of empathy at work. You can literally feel their pain. You are meant to feel empathy for the suffering of others as it moves you to action, but it should not be action to fix. It is only your own deep sense of disconnection that keeps you from feeling empathy for everyone. You've chosen a complex and difficult reality. There are an infinite number of others as you will eventually remember.

It is important that you as a parent or loved one take care of yourself and honor your own guidelines. If you allow your loved one to cross boundaries that you would never cross yourself in your own home then you dishonor yourself. In effect you are saying he or she is more important than you. You may believe that, but it is not true. Every human being is equally important whether they be a prince or a pauper. You all affect everything else equally. My parents never kicked me out of the house although they moved me into a tent in the yard after they caught me using shortly after my first rehab experience. What drove them insane was my lying about being straight when even to a two-year-old it was clear I was altered. You are never responsible, for you can never choose for someone else. You may think you can and it may appear that you did, but whether a person is conscious of their choice or not, **THEY** choose. You can believe this now or you can wait until you get here where you will be shown it is true. No soul can force another soul to choose against its will. Me as Split Jeans can never tell your Ripped Pants what to do. There are no hierarchies where I am now, nor should there be where you are now.

Acceptance, as I have described it, is the key to having any influence at all in the direction you would like your loved one to go. You can support them in their efforts to get clean, but do not judge their choice to use in the first place. You may hate it, but don't judge it. You are not living their lives, you are living your own. You believe they are destroying their lives and it certainly appears to be the case, but they are playing a role with purpose. You both make choices in each and every moment based on your level of awareness and the operative belief at the time. His or her purpose or role is not your role or your purpose. Anthony Hopkins in the audience is not booing and screaming at Hannibal Lecter, and urging medical intervention. My father eventually got to that point of acceptance when he could calmly ask me where I went when I nodded off. Me as David however, didn't accept me, but I sure as hell experienced the unusual, which was my intent in coming into physical reality in the first place.

There is also a big difference between caring and being concerned. My parents always cared for me, but were also concerned and worried about me when I began using. Here's the difference. You will always care about what is important to you, whether they be people you love or principles you hold dear. Concern, when directed at people is a discounting of their choices.

The Horse Rode Me

Again, it is you saying you know better what they should be choosing. You do not. To break your pattern of trying to save or to fix you must shift your attention to yourself. You are consumed with paying attention to your loved one. What is he doing? What is she feeling? Stop! The question you must ask is what are <u>you</u> doing and what are <u>you</u> feeling and where is <u>your</u> attention directed, and how is your loved one reflecting <u>you</u>.

I'll use myself and my mother as an example. She liked me calling her Mama so I will refer to her henceforth as Mama. Even when I was sober, she worried about me, wanting for me what all loving mothers want for their sons and daughters, health, happiness and no stress. She knew that stress could throw me into a relapse and Mama also knew that I did everything "balls to the wall." She knew if I relapsed it would mean the end of me. So, while I was still alive my Mama's ultimate worry was that I would relapse. In turning her attention to herself, she should have asked what my relapse would mean to her. I know that she would answer by saying what it might result in for me, but that is not the question here. I was and always had been the only one responsible for me. It is difficult even today for Mama to answer that question without involving me in her answer. Her children are the center of her Universe. If you have lost a child it would be difficult for you as well. Maybe her answer and yours as well might be that you would not be able to deal with the grief of losing your child. Your child loses nothing...trust me on this.

For you to understand how important YOU are I need to press home this point. You are where you are for you, and in paying attention to you everyone else is aided as well. Everyone else, while also there for themselves, is also there for you. There is no end, just as there is no beginning. You all existed before choosing physical reality on Earth. Just as Anthony Hopkins has played many roles, his number pales in comparison to yours. You, out of all the potential mothers on the planet, was the one your child chose. **<u>You never let your child down for it was never possible for you to do so.</u>**

The Horse Rode Me

You Have Been What You Love And What You Hate

I am going to tell you only a small part of the complexity of who you are and why comparing yourself to others is a waste of your energy. Most of you in the Western world believe in 'one and done,' while the East adheres to a belief in reincarnation. You are both right and wrong in that what it is you each believe gets you into the target zone, but quite far from the bull's eye. This information can help you in your current manifestation of you by way of expanding your current low sense of connection and diminishing your desire to be like someone else. Let me remind you, however, that wanting to change is natural, while judging (not accepting) who you currently are is not.

There is no difference between you and your soul. You are one and the same. Your soul is not one thing and you are just part of its imagination. With that in mind I am not going to use the pronoun 'your' when referring to soul. Imagine you <u>as</u> soul and give soul a name. Mine, as you now know, I've named Split Jeans. My friends Emily B and Emily H and Steve and Ben will get it. So will Becky. Now, imagine soul (you) as a dandelion ready to caste its seeds into the wind, but think of the landing zone as time and space. Each of soul's thousands of seeds, cast forth simultaneously, will find purchase in a different time and a different location, some close in time and location and others eons apart. To Split Jeans (me) all time is simultaneous. It is not linear as it appears to you. This is where the East misses the bull's eye. I have had 2,842 lives simultaneously in the past, present and future. The point of this is not the simultaneous time bit, for that in and of itself is too much for you to wrap your mind around. The point is that you have experienced it all.

You want to be tall? You already are tall. You want to be rich? You already are rich. You want to be white, black, brown, yellow or red? You already are. If you are a white racist and reading this, you are in this very moment black and are being horribly abused by your white slave owner. You get to experience everything, and you experience it all now. You experience the hatred of a white man as a black man. That is true empathy. You have been an abused waitress and the abuser of the waitress. You might well ask how does knowing this help the me that I know as me now? If you can believe what I am sharing with you here and employ the rules of the game then the choices you make will be more likely to get you directly across the street. You will not need to travel the circumference of the globe to cross the street as I did, unless you consciously choose to do so. You will no longer need to sweat the small stuff, as the expression goes. You will be more prone to remain in the now, which is the only place from which you have any power. You will not have to get where I am and say as Chris O'Connor and I said, WTF, along with a palm plant to your ethereal forehead.

You are concurrently experiencing the highest of highs and the lowest of lows. There is nothing to judge, but everything to experience. You have been (are) more evil than you can imagine and more saintly than Jesus himself. When he said "I and the Father are one," he had a breakthrough insight of the connectedness of all things. He was telling me that David and Split Jeans are one and the same and that all of consciousness is ONE. It is the ONE that you refer to as God. You swim in the One, and the ONE is constantly expanding, constantly evolving. The ONE can never be a 'done deal'. You are already on a trip that makes the

The Horse Rode Me

most mind-expanding acid trip seem like a mere walk across the street.

Think about something you learned to dislike, or even hate, early in your life. Keep in mind that you chose your parents and therefore your geographical and time insertion point. Let's say that you were born in what you refer to as the reddest red area of Alabama. Your parents were Southern Baptists, which means before choosing them there was a great probability that you too would be brought up in the same church. They also happened to be members of the KKK. Now remember, from the point from which you made your selection of parents you knew many of the probabilities from which you would be choosing, but you are seeing them from a perfectly neutral and accepting place. Another you chooses exactly opposite probabilities in a closely adjacent time. That you was born to liberal, college educated parents in Massachusetts. You and the other you are still One, but under the game rules you learn to hate each other because you have left behind your memory of who you are. You are literally hating yourself. He's a liberal snowflake and you're a racist redneck. A good example considering the times you live in…right?

The rule of forgetting is in the process of being dropped. In other words, one of the game rules is being changed after many thousands of linear-time years. You are all slowly awakening to who you are and where you came from, but for now let's go back to the time before you read my book and look at the AA Twelve Steps. If Bill Wilson's Twelve Step program is working for you don't change it. I am addressing those of you that struggle staying clean using the twelve-step program
'm going to look at the steps through the lens of what you have read so far.

The Horse Rode Me

The Horse Rode Me

The Horse Rode Me

Twelve Steps: A Different Look

Step One: We admit we are powerless over Alcohol and that our lives have become unmanageable.
You are never powerless unless you believe you are powerless. What it is you believe drives everything you experience. This is where your power lies. If you believe you are a helpless victim of a drug then you can absolutely count on that being true for you. As for your life being unmanageable, it is being perfectly managed by you. You might not like it, as I didn't like it, but it is you managing it. No one else is calling the shots for you, not Soul and certainly not God. It is all you as Soul and as ONE. You may believe you have lost control of your life, but I assure you that there is purpose in what you have created for yourself. Now, when I tell you that your beliefs drive your experience, I am referring to beliefs without any doubt. If you say I believe I can fly, and jump out of a plane without a chute, I assure you that you will be joining me here very shortly. It is on your beliefs that you must work.

Step Two: Came to believe that a Power greater than ourselves could restore us to sanity.
Step one right off the bat asks you to believe (which you probably already do) that you are powerless. Sure, you believe you have the power over some things in your life, but certainly not all things and certainly not heroin. You have the power to turn your vehicle right or left, but it wasn't you that chose to have a front

wheel blowout at 70 MPH. Maybe it was God or maybe it was bad luck, but it sure as hell wasn't you. Step two continues to take away your power by placing it in a "Higher Power's" hands, or worse, in 'Shit Happens' hands. Accidents and luck, whether good or bad, is controlled by someone or something else in your current beliefs. You have been taught this from your earliest days. Despite what you currently think about yourself, you are sane. You simply don't know who you are.

Step Three: Made a decision to turn our will and our lives over to the care of God as we understand Him.

If you can imagine a bigger God than the one you currently imagine, don't you think that God can top your imagination. The way you currently conceive of your God is based on a prior and even stronger belief that you are a separate being stuck on a planet that came together by way of happenstance. Trust me when I tell you that sitting back and allowing God to run your life is not going to work. You have created God in your own image and not the reverse. God, or ONE as I now prefer to call God, has given you free will. You have given yourself free will. ONE is not a puppet master. Any changes in your life are because of you. You just don't realize you are the cause. Having said that, you are all connected, and as you change your beliefs about yourself you will draw to you the reflection of that change. Thank your conception of God if you wish, but more importantly thank yourself, for you ARE your conception of God. Everything will respond to your appreciation of self. Everything you believe to be true will be reflected to you.

Step Four: Made a searching and moral inventory of ourselves.

This is something you all should be doing on a regular basis, but the moral inventory should be based on your individual inner guidelines, and what it is you believe. What is moral for you may not be necessarily moral for everyone. If you are religious and have accepted your religion's version of morality there is nothing wrong with this. The introspection then would be about how you have broken those individual guidelines. With that introspection should come non-judgment not only of yourself, but an understanding that you as soul does not judge either. Soul also does not judge anyone else. You may actually find that you do not hold all of your religion's teachings as part of your own list of guidelines. For instance, many religions consider abortion and homosexuality to be sins against God. If you have had an abortion or are homosexual you may not hold this teaching as an individual guideline. If you do hold them it will be difficult to accept yourself under any conditions. Any religious guideline that makes you judge yourself or another is probably not one of your inner guidelines. You can feel within you what your true guidelines are. Whether you do or do not hold these guidelines, the key is the understanding that they are yours and do not need to be adhered to by those that do not hold them. Therein lies acceptance, which includes non-judgment. Remember, you do not need to like that which you accept. You may not like that you have broken one or more of your guidelines, but you must accept without judgment, that you did.

Step Five: Admitted to God, to ourselves, and to another human being the exact nature of our wrongs.

There are no wrongs! There are only choices. In the eyes of the culture in which you reside, however, there appears to you that there are wrongs. No other person knows the path you have chosen to explore as this version of you. You probably don't know either, but that is because you have not been paying attention to you. Your focus has been outward rather than inward. As an addict you probably have done more things you didn't want to do than the average person. Guilt, as I've stated, can be a killer. It takes your focus completely out of the now and castes it into the past. You have no power there. Remember, Anthony Hopkins does not judge Hannibal Lecter. Soul doesn't judge itself as you. Neither should you. If you didn't like something you did in the past, choose differently in the Now. The Now is all you have. If you desire to acknowledge the wrongs against your own guidelines then do so. It will have a cathartic effect. But, leave out the self-judgment. Acceptance does not need to include liking. It does however, need to exclude judgment.

Step Six: We are entirely ready to have God remove all these defects of character.

Is it any wonder that the Twelve Steps are less successful than they are successful when they see you as crawling with defects? Anthony Hopkins no more sees Hannibal Lecter as flawed as Soul sees you. Split Jeans and I are ONE. Your current conception of God is actually better defined as Soul/you. The 'real' God is beyond conception. He is the twig that snaps when you step upon it. She is the water that bathes you and quenches your thirst. It is the Universe that surrounds you. God is everything and no thing. God is the defect AA claims you have. I know that sounds strange, but if everything is GOD then so are what we think of as defects.

Step Seven: Humbly ask him to remove our shortcomings.

Shortcomings only exist in your mind and because your mind actually expands God, there can be no shortcomings. This is not to say there are things you would like to change about yourself. This is natural. It is called expansion. Even things you do that you 'believe' diminishes you, actually expands you, for you have now experienced something you have not experienced before. Notice the word 'humbly.' God is not Caligula or Nero or Louis XIV. If the God that you believe in has a tantrum over a lack of humility on your part you might want to reformulate your concept of God. Make your God bigger. Don't wait until you get here.

Step Eight: Made a list of all persons we had harmed, and became willing to make amends to them all.

When I was still with you and understood reality as you do, my list was as long as a Giraffe's neck. Much of what I did under that thinking was emotional harm although on occasion it was physical. I did not know that those I 'harmed' got as much from me as I got from them. Remember, we all draw to each other exactly what we need in the moment whether it be 'good' or 'bad.' Often you learn as much, if not more, from the bad as you do from the good. In any event making amends can be of benefit for it can assuage your feelings of guilt. If it makes you feel good then do it, but include acceptance of self in the process.

Step Nine: Made direct amends to such people wherever possible, except when to do so would injure them or others.

Let's say you make amends to an individual who didn't know that you stole from them. Let's further assume that by doing so they judge you. Now that you understand that by judging another you judge yourself, you may want to rethink making your amends to this particular individual. The majority of you that are still breathing continue to judge when you are offended in one way or another. It is currently most likely that making amends will often solidify their belief that drug addicts are bad. If you are going to make amends, do it for yourself. You cannot choose what the person you make amends to will do, but you can choose what you will do. Hopefully it will raise your sense of self-worth that both you and your culture had tried so hard to squash.

Step Ten: Continued to take personal inventory and when we were wrong promptly admitted it.

There's that word 'wrong' again. If you stay present in the moment and simply take inventory of your surroundings, you'll be ok. Taking inventory of recent wrongs (whatever that is) engages your Monkey Mind and tosses you into the past. You can learn to be present in each moment. When you are, you will be consciously aware and thus be less likely to commit what you feel is a wrong. Here's what you might think about doing. Write down all the things you consider to be your inner guidelines. As an example, here are a few of mine: 1) Don't do to someone else what you don't want them to do to you. 2) Don't judge what you know nothing about. I struggled with this one many times. 3) Be kind. 4) Stand up for the underdog. I was pretty good at this one. 5) Encourage those I felt need encouragement. These are just a few. What I can tell you from my current perspective is that putting yourself first should be your primary guideline. By putting others before yourself is actually a devaluation of who you are. It's like saying, "I am not worthy enough to put myself first." Having said that, when you finally come to a realization of your own value and worth you will have no difficulty valuing others.

Step Eleven: Sought through prayer and meditation to improve our conscious contact with God as we understand Him, praying only for knowledge of His will for us and the power to carry that out.

What this really comes down to is paying attention, as His/Hers/Its will for you is really yours. You made the decision to come into this world with a definite goal of exploring a particular issue/concept. Everything you have ever experienced has been by your own choice and in alignment with what you came here to explore. That you have traveled around the globe to cross the street is only because you have not paid attention to yourself and have ignored your inner senses...maybe that is what your plan was all along. As long as you see yourself as a victim of others or of circumstance and then blame others and circumstance for your condition you will never know the precise purpose of your visit here. You have the tools to know. You merely need to wake up to the reality of who you are.

Step Twelve: Having had a spiritual awakening as the result of these steps, we tried to carry this message to alcoholics, and to practice these principles in all our affairs.

A spiritual awakening is an awakening to the knowledge of who you are. The rules you have been following are not the rules of the game you have agreed to participate in. Any rule that you follow that tells you that you are 'less than' is a rule you must ditch. Any concept that says that the existence of the planet and you are mere happenstance should be ditched. This is the current materialist view. Any belief that says you are separate from everything else needs to be tossed in the trash heap. You are and always have been connected to everything. You are a pearl among pearls, a gem like no other.

Relapses

My father just finished listening to the popular podcast called

The Horse Rode Me

Dopey, a great podcast for active, in recovery and clean addicts. The book was finished. But the podcast triggered an impulse to my father, with my assist, to add this section right after my comments on the twelve steps. In the podcast the guest was talking about long term suboxone use as a valid addiction treatment and linked it to diabetics using long term insulin injections to manage their diabetes. The guest also linked relapses to those who have been cancer free for years and then the cancer reappeared. I want to look at both cancer and dope relapses as motivators. The initial onset of both cancer and addiction as well as the relapses are actually motivators for change. If you can believe much of what I have to say here, particularly regarding creating all of your experience, you will get what I have to say about relapses as motivators.

Under your current understanding of reality, you tell yourself that both cancer and addiction was not something you chose. It makes sense to you logically because what sane person would choose such things. Two things here to consider: 1) the main directive of consciousness is to expand and 2) each of you comes into the world with a particular intent to explore. All of you get stuck and begin spinning your wheels. Think of a hamster running on that circular wheel running hard and getting nowhere. You have already given yourself more subtle motivators, but you paid no attention to them. Think of motivators as someone gently knocking on your door. He knows you're inside, but you ignore the knock. He knocks harder. Still you don't respond. Eventually he breaks down the door. Breaking down the door can be likened to cancer, drug addiction and relapses to both. I heard the softer motivators over and over prior to creating my own addiction and relapses, but ignored them. I had to get out the big guns.

Cancer and addiction turns you around when crossing the street. Maybe you get a quarter of the way around the globe before turning back to cross the street directly. Sometimes, like me, you travel the full globe to get across the street. Motivators require a change in life direction, especially those that break down the door to get your attention. They may change you for a while, but then you get in your stuck zone again and go deaf to the softer motivators. Relapses come from inattention and a refusal to move. Looking back on my life I can see how much drug addiction expanded me in terms of opening me up and expanding my consciousness by way of acceptance, empathy and compassion. Had I followed an early drive to acquire lots of money I would have lived a life unfulfilled. Recall, my first journal post: *Dear Tooth Fairy,*

I lost my tooth and it did fall out so you still have to give me the money.

I suppose that should have been a clue. Those who have survived cancer and addiction will attest that their disease changed them in many positive ways. The sledge hammers are designed to crack you open.

The Horse Rode Me

Getting Deeper Into Beliefs

Previously I just brushed the surface of beliefs, but now it is time to go deeper into them and their power. It will be difficult for you to change your circumstances without fully understanding the power of what it is you believe. Currently, but this is changing quickly, most of you believe that your external world preexists what you believe about it. That is to say, first there is a world and then there is you to perceive it. NEWSFLASH! You are not what you perceive yourself to be. What you see is what you believe about yourself. What this means is that there is no correct way to perceive your world or your experiences, although the general structure of your world is an agreed upon construction. You perceive exactly what <u>you</u> project, and what you project is your feedback loop about yourself.

To avoid mass insanity there are also mass creations upon which most of you agree. The world is a globe, gravity, night and day, fire is hot and ice is cold are just a few of the mass agreements/beliefs. That two people can meet at Starbucks at a specific location at a specific time is the result of those mass agreements, and includes time. Anthony Hopkins could not have played his roles if the set was different for all the other actors in the movies and time was different for all the actors. As for individual beliefs and perception you can think of them as the film that feeds the projector that casts the image upon a screen. Your beliefs are the film and your perception is the projector. What you experience is the screen, a very real three-dimensional screen. When a group of two or five or eleven people see an apple fall from a tree, they will agree that an apple fell from a specific tree. However, each individual creates their own apple and their own tree. They may argue about the color of the apple and the leaves of the tree, but the truth is that they are all accurate in their descriptions. There are no preexisting apples or trees aside from each individual perception. Only energy exists and perception coalesces it into form. Each person is correct in their description.

Europe uses heroin as a pain management tool for cancer patients and yet those patients that are cured have not become addicted. In their culture they have a strongly held belief that if heroin is used for pain management the patient will not become addicted. In the US you don't hold that belief and so I had an anal cyst removed without any anesthesia. I dared not risk the chance of a relapse. They also believe that addiction will occur if used outside the medical paradigm of pain management. What I am saying here is that there is nothing special about the chemical makeup of cancer patients in Europe that protects them from addiction. It is their strongly held belief that keeps them safe. The key word here is 'strongly.' When I was eighteen my father shared with me the story of Harvard psychologist Richard Alpert. The story pertains to what I have just shared with you.

While at Harvard Alpert began dabbling in the use of LSD. His experiences with the drug led him to believe that the drug was the 'Holy Grail' to unlocking the secrets of reality. In 1967 he left Harvard and undertook a pilgrimage to India to share his 'discovery' with various Hindu gurus. What eventually changed irrevocably his understanding of the human condition was a meeting he had with an old diminutive guru. Believing LSD to be the end all and cure all of human suffering he asked this guru to take a tab of LSD. It was enough, Alpert thought, to give the guru

The Horse Rode Me

the trip of a lifetime. The tab had no effect on the guru. He offered a second tab and then a third, enough to take down a Rhino. The old guru merely shrugged his shoulders and said, "not as good as meditation." This shook Alpert to his core. He stayed in India, converted to Hinduism and became the man you may know as Ram Dass (Servant of God). He returned to the US and in 1971 published his best seller Be Here Now.

The point I am trying to convey in this story is not the power of Alpert's religious conversion, but rather the power of the guru's beliefs, or lack thereof. First, he had little or no knowledge of LSD and a strong, almost absolute, belief in the power of meditation. Secondly, by way of his lifelong practice of meditation he had a very different understanding of the human condition. What I am getting at is that the LSD holds no power in and of itself, but rather works as a focal point for the real generator of the experience, one's belief. Let's dive even deeper into the subject of beliefs.

Before you come into this world you contain all beliefs. Look at it as the most complete tool box you can imagine. You decide the time period and then your parents, which includes the geographic area where you will be born. This, by default, will include the cultural beliefs of your parents and the area of the world in which they live. These are all chosen based on what it is you desire to explore in this particular life. You remove from the tool box those initial beliefs you will need and will serve you, but you bring the full tool box with you. Once born you will immediately forget that you have in your possession your most valuable asset, the full tool box. If you are reading this you have inherited the modern age beliefs, two of which tells you that you can be a victim and that the reality you were born into preexisted your entry into it.

One of the side effects of just these two beliefs is that you have become victims of the world in which you live. You have erected enormous systems of protection, and why wouldn't you with beliefs such as the two I mentioned above. You have so little confidence in your body's ability to protect and heal itself you have erected one of your world's most profitable industries. Every time you pop a pill you are sending a message to your body that you do not trust it to do its job effectively. Left to its own devices the body could deal with any self-created illness or disease, but it is exquisitely responsive to your beliefs.

On December 18, 2018 my father was watching the CBS Evening News. A segment appeared that told the story of an eleven-year-old girl's miraculous disappearance of a rare, inoperable brain tumor known as a diffuse intrinsic pontine glioma. It was diagnosed in June of the same year. There is no cure for this tumor and less than 1% survive beyond five years. It is a very nasty killing disease. Radiation is the treatment of choice, but not a cure. Two months into the treatment her MRI showed no evidence of a tumor…none. Her doctor could not explain the disappearance of her tumor. These things we generally call miracles because they go against what we think we know about reality. Beliefs hold the power to create and un-create.

The engine of creation in your world is beliefs. This is the reason hypnotism can be so effective. It transplants a more beneficial belief for one that is creating trauma in your life. As long as you hold these beliefs as truth you better continue taking your medications and seeing your doctors. Be of good faith however, as these hardened beliefs you refer to as truths will eventually fade as you all awaken to who you are. But you will continue to generate your individual and mass reality by way of your beliefs. Your beliefs become self-fulfilling. It is important to know that thought does not create your beliefs, but rather is influenced by them.

One major belief you will have to supplant is your belief in Cause and Effect that says reality is the cause while the belief is the effect. <u>It is reality that changes in response to your beliefs</u>. Understanding this changes everything. Since everything is connected, nothing changes in isolation. Everything affects everything else, and as you change yourself the mass belief is also changed. I cannot say this enough, REALITY CONFORMS TO YOUR BELIEFS ABOUT IT. The reality you create is real. Don't lose sight of that. It simply does not operate in the way you currently believe it does. There are a limitless number of beliefs in your tool box. That is necessary in a world created by the beliefs of those that populate it. Think of the artist Renoir creating his masterpieces using only primary colors. All great artists were wizards at mixing colors to create a wholly new color. You too are a wizard, but your canvas is reality itself. Renoir uses paints. You use beliefs. Drop the ones that cause you grief and replace it with ones that bring you joy. I'll tell you later how to do that.

Facts Are Strongly Held Beliefs

Scientists will tell you their discoveries are not beliefs. They are facts. They will also tell you that your religious stories are not facts, but beliefs or at best symbols or markers pointing to something else. In the West you live in a postmodern age where you place your faith in the findings of science...unless you happen to be a religious fundamentalist, or someone whose education has been woefully underdone. There is no correct thing you should believe. Fundamentalists beliefs serve them as well in their exploration as your scientific beliefs serve you in yours, and many don't think of science or religion at all. Remember, you are all connected and everything influences everything else. So, don't be too righteous about the correctness of your beliefs in relation to the beliefs of others. I-am-right-and-you- are-wrong thinking has severely polarized you. There is no more-right just as there is no less-right. They are choices of beliefs. You can choose to believe what I am telling you now, or you can wait to join me and give a big WTF as I did and as Chris did. Strongly held beliefs are what you currently call facts.

Let's look at some of your beliefs about food. You can't help but have noticed that the information you get seems to change almost every day. Butter was good, then it was bad and then it was good again. Whole milk was good, then it was bad. Skim milk was good then almond milk was better because of the vegan movement. Fat was bad and then some fats were good. Animal fat tastes great, but killing the animals raised in mega industrial farms was bad. I could fill the rest of this book with beliefs about food. You will never hear me say, "they are just beliefs" because the beliefs actually are your reality. Your reality is as real as it gets, but it is you that is creating it. If you don't like what you are creating, change your beliefs.

Many years ago my father told me how Dan Rather just killed a countless number of bald men. I didn't watch much news then so my father had to explain who Dan Rather was. He went on to say that Rather announced that scientists discovered a link between male pattern baldness and heart disease. I shrugged my shoulders, having no idea what in the hell he was talking about. He explained that there are enough bald men that have such strong beliefs in the power of science that they now believe they will be the victims of heart disease. They don't realize that it is the strength of their belief that will create the disease. Years later I remembered that conversation. I was using and had yet to get clean. Death was on my mind often in those days. Death always hovers above an addict's head, one syringe away from lowering its boom. I think we all know this, and because of it develop deep and lasting friendships. I carried around a lot of regret and grief, losing more friends to heroin than you can count on your fingers and toes, but the ones that stuck with me I will always cherish. After telling me the Dan Rather story he said to be careful of what it is I believe. I should have taken his words to heart. I was pretty much consumed with where my next fix would come from and how I'd get the money for it. It usually wasn't from work.

Your body responds to what you **believe** about the food you ingest and not the food itself. Hard to believe, right? It's true, but if you want to be healthy the best method would be to trust your body and its immune system to do the job it was born to do. The same holds for any addictive substance, even heroin. Some people are easily addicted and others not. Your science says that the reason you are easily addicted is because of opioid receptors in your brain. But the truth is this, and it gets to the age-old question, 'what came first the chicken or the egg.' Yes, there are opiate receptors in your brain, but they appeared after you installed your beliefs about heroin. You are like Richard Alpert before he became Ram Dass. You might want to think about becoming the Guru. He didn't need LSD to get high on life. It's best to get high on life and not on Heroin. It is possible.

The Horse Rode Me

The Horse Rode Me

Belief Systems

There are numberless beliefs that you carry in your tool box. For ease of reference they all fall within several belief systems, some of which I will describe here. It is important to know this if you are to begin working with what is in your tool box

Good/Bad...Better/Worse
This is the most pervasive of belief systems as it weaves its way in and out of all the other belief systems. All of your likes and dislikes fall within this belief system. It is also the belief system to which you attach your judgments. Keep in mind that Split Pants (Soul) does not judge, and neither should you. Your likes and dislikes and your goods and bads should not carry judgments, which is to say that what is good or bad for you should not lead to the assumption that your good or bad is a universal truth. Your individual goods and bads only apply to you, although many others may share them with you. An easy example of this would be what is evolving within your politics. As my father is typing these words there is a battle raging over an appointment to the Supreme Court in America. Many of you hold strong opinions whether Kavanaugh should be confirmed or not. The addition of Dr. Ford's sex assault allegations intensified both positions to confirm or not to confirm. Each side strongly judges the other and the polarization intensifies.

I remind you that you are all playing your individual roles, but that each of you affects everyone and everything else. When you judge another, you are also judging yourself. You are all reflections of each other. In this particular Supreme Court situation my father is a good example of implementing what I am saying in our book. He understands that his feelings on this matter are his and holds no one else to abide by them. I can tell you that if he was the lone wolf howling in the wilderness of opposition, he would not fight to convince the world that he is right. That is not to say he would not share his position, for he would and does. Regarding the matter at hand he dislikes the opposing position, but understands that those holding it are but playing their own role in their own play, which is also his. He will discuss his position, but not with the intent to convince or instruct. If he is an influence, he knows that it is only by the choice of the other individual to accept it. He has likes and dislikes on the issues and the role players. The difference is that he accepts it all. Split Jeans (me) knew he 'got' this acceptance thing when he calmly asked me where I went when nodding off. There was no screaming. No judgment. Just acceptance. He didn't like that I was using, but in that moment I knew he was in total acceptance of me.

The same holds true for all your preferences and guidelines. Look at the Pro Life and Pro-Choice proponents. This played a critical role in the Kavanaugh debacle. I use the word debacle in the sense that you would describe it. Soul does not see it as so. It doesn't matter which side you are on, Soul sees it as neutral. God does not need soldiers or proselytizers, for she IS the soldiers and proselytizers. Neither does a fetus. If it is your choice to defend a fetus do so, but I am telling you that if it is the choice of that fetus to be born he will be born. If it is the choice of that fetus to be aborted, nothing you do can block that choice. Ultimately you cannot choose for another, including the fetus. If you are Pro-Life then don't have an abortion. It's as simple as that. If you are Pro-Choice I am telling you that you cannot choose for the fetus any more than you can choose for the mother. If that fetus chooses to be born it will be born. The Fetus is as much Soul as I was Split Jeans at the time I was a fetus.

Duality plays a part in this belief system of good/bad, better/worse. Up/down, in/out/ under/over, tall/short, fat/skinny, strong/weak, smart/stupid, light/heavy are all aspects of duality. There are many more. Choosing which you prefer is an aspect of the belief system. Without duality there would be no conscious discernment. Without duality in your world you could not develop preferences. The belief system of good/bad, better worse works

The Horse Rode Me

like this. The fact that you prefer beauty over ugly is the belief system. That there is beauty and ugliness is a function of duality. That you like the smell of a rose and don't like the smell of a dog turd is the belief system, while the odors of a rose and dog turd are a function of duality. That you like a person who is not on drugs and dislike a person who is on drugs is a function of the belief system, while straight and stoned is a function of duality. The truth is that they are all neutral, merely two sides of the same coin. It is your choosing that gives them a charge. You will always choose, and all of your choices are driven by what it is you believe. The important thing to remember is that no one else on the planet has to choose the same as you. Many will and do, but you must accept those that don't. You don't have to like them, but you do need to drop the judgment you attach to them. <u>That</u> is Acceptance.

All of your moral and ethical choices are a function of this belief system of good/bad, better/worse. If you are Jewish, not eating pork is good. If you are Catholic sexual thoughts must be confessed. Gluttony is a sin, while moderation is believed to be good. A big one is that selfishness is bad and selflessness is good. At one time (a very long time) eating meat on Friday was a bad thing if you were Catholic, and then, all of a sudden it didn't matter. For Mormons polygamy was good and now it is bad. You place so many judgments on yourself for not being or doing what is officially accepted by your culture. You **ARE** your culture. You are part of the ones that create your officially accepted reality. When you judge yourself, you are expressing your individual battles with this belief system. THE BELIEF SYSTEM IS NEUTRAL! Just ask Anthony Hopkins about himself as Hannibal Lecter. You as Soul does not judge anything you do, and you ARE Soul, just as I am Split Jeans. It is the Monkey Mind that judges. It is you that chooses. That is going to be a huge WTF for you when you are done with your experience on earth…unless you get it before you pass on.

Think of this and all belief systems as trees, each one as large as the home tree in the movie Avatar. Now think of the individual

The Horse Rode Me

beliefs within each system as the near limitless number of leaves on the tree. When you accept an individual belief (turn it neutral) it falls to the ground and therefore loses its hold on you. But it grows back immediately upon falling. You rightly ask why? Acceptance or non-acceptance happens in each and every moment of your life. Were that leaf never to grow back it would limit choice. It must always be available to choose or not choose. A diseased leaf is as valuable as a pristine leaf. Your world is filled with two religious admonitions. Thou shalt and Thou shalt not. At times the first has you doing things you don't want to do such as baby sitting your daughter's child when you are exhausted or have made other plans. At other times you may be perfectly happy to do so. The second, at times, keeps you from doing something you want to do such as sleeping in on Sunday rather than going to church. Either choice is neutral. They are merely choices. You can align with a belief or not for you all have preferences and guidelines. This is the freedom of choice. Your Bible calls it Free Will. Remember, however, that good is as much a judgment as bad. When you accept a belief, you hold no judgment regarding your choice or the choice of others. When this happens, you will begin the process of accepting differences and desist from comparing yourself to others. You are not better OR worse when you don't do a Thou Shalt or when you do a Thou Shalt Not. You simply ARE.

The Horse Rode Me

The Belief System of Truths

Here is the paradox of truths, better known to you as facts. Since beliefs drive your perception that is then projected outwardly as your physical reality, they hold the power of truth. Eventually, if enough people begin to hold the same belief it spreads to the point of becoming a fact. It becomes real not only to those believing it, but by the general population as well. If the belief spreads that a turd facial rejuvenates the skin to the point that it becomes a mass belief, then you can be sure it will rejuvenate your skin. I'm sure you are all relieved that drinking your own urine has health benefits never caught on. You are all connected and beliefs can spread. And so, you all begin playing the same film. Until, that is, someone inserts a new opposing belief that gathers converts, so to speak. The opposing belief gathers steam and itself spreads to the point that the old fact is discarded and the new is inserted into the mass consciousness. When a belief becomes a truth we act upon it automatically, and when we act automatically freedom of choice becomes constricted. Truth, therefore, in your reality is not as consequential as your belief systems, for it is your beliefs that create your truths.

A strongly held belief since the philosopher Herbert Spencer first proposed it is the belief in the survival of the fittest. In this, only the strongest of a species thrives and passes on its genes, thus ensuring the survival of the species. It is a belief of predator and prey and dominance. You have incorporated this belief into a definition of yourselves. For many it was and is held as a fact. Here is a belief you can incorporate as a fact and the sooner you make it a truth in your world the less you will feel disconnected. You live in a world of cooperation, not one of competition. As more of you take on this belief the more of you will be attracted to it. The more it becomes a mass held fact the more the world will reflect the truth of it back to you. You are always given the proof of your beliefs whether it be good or bad as you define those terms. Beliefs are neutral. You assign judgment to them, just don't hold everyone else to those you adhere to. Competition supports separation while cooperation supports connection.

Nothing travels faster than the speed of light...no longer a fact

Einstein believed in cause and effect. He could not bring himself to believe that probabilities ruled your world. His theory of relativity postulated that nothing travels faster than the speed of light. Trust me when I tell you that it is important for you to understand what it is I am going to tell you here. You do not need to be a quantum physicist to make sense of it. One of the tenets of quantum theory is that of non-locality, the ability to communicate over any distance instantly. The notion of non-locality parted with Einstein's claim that nothing traveled faster than the speed of light. Your closest star, Alpha Proxima, is four light years away from you. This simply means that the light of Alpha Proxima takes four years to reach your eyes. What you see when you look at this star is four-years-old. In other words, when you look at your night sky you are looking into the past. If Alpha Proxima were to blow up today you would not see it until four years had passed. Einstein readily agreed with my last comment.

Keep in mind that quantum physics deals with the smallest of particles. The atom compared to a quanta is like Mount Everest compared to a grain of sand. All of the technologies you so much appreciate today is the result of the study of these smallest of

KNOWN particles. What Einstein tried and ultimately failed in refuting involved spontaneously decaying particles. Here is my simple explanation of what happens when a particle spontaneously decays. When a particle decays let's look at two aspects of the particle and call them A and B. They can be anywhere...that is until either A or B is observed. Once the observation takes place, let's say of aspect B, the unobserved particle A is always found in exactly the opposite direction. What bothered Einstein was that it <u>instantly</u> appears in the opposite direction. The idea of non-locality, the instantaneous appearance of particle A, flies in the face of Einstein's postulation that nothing travels faster that the speed of light. Even the speed of light includes the ideas of time and space. It takes time for the light of Alpha Proxima to travel through space to reach your eyes. Not particle A once particle B is observed. It is instant.

I won't get into the history of the arguments that ensued in the field of quantum physics to either prove or disprove Einstein's belief that nothing travels faster than the speed of light other than to say that in the early 1980's Einstein was proved wrong. French physicist Alain Aspect conducted a series of experiments that proved there were no hidden variables that allowed A to communicate its position to B before being detected. The position of A when B was observed was instant, even if A appeared at the farthest reaches of our universe. This was a problem for Einstein who saw the universe as a collection of separate parts, i.e., A was separate from B. What I am trying to impress upon all of you is that you are all connected in a unified whole. In other words, you and the father are one. You are never alone except for what your mind tells you. It is a belief that you must replace. Addicts feel hopelessly alone and stuck in a hell that current therapies are inadequate to resolve. You are playing an incredibly real role. I am telling you that you are so much more than you believe yourselves to be. You are the head of the spear but don't know it...yet.

Fear
Fear is as big a player in your belief systems as strength is in

weight lifting. Most of you love security, safety and sameness. For many, change poses a threat. The problem here is that consciousness is all about change. It abhors stagnation. You, ultimately being consciousness, will initiate a motivator that will dislodge you from your stuck place. You may not believe you created the motivation for change because you have not been paying attention to yourselves, and, as the saying goes, you believe 'shit happens'. Your fondness of security, sameness and safety is based on fear...fear of the unknown. When you concentrate on fear you will draw what it is you fear toward you, and if the fear is strong enough you will experience what you fear. Fear is a speculation of things or actions not present. Fear in the Now (your actual momentary experience) serves a valuable purpose and when you hear the distinct sound of a rattlesnake it stops you in your tracks and out of the range of the snake's fangs.

Illness is a commonly chosen motivator. You do not believe you chose it because you do not understand who you are nor the rules of the game you are playing. What you believe is that you are a victim of illness or bad health. Both are feared, and thus many embark on beliefs that you **Believe** will give you protection from both. You start popping supplements, eating kale and flax seed, drinking eight glasses of water each day, getting eight hours of sleep each night, getting weekly shots to keep allergies at bay, and increase your exercise routines if you had any to begin with. What do those beliefs say to your body? In answering that question remember that the body is exquisitely responsive to what you believe about it. What it tells your body is that without everything I mentioned above, it will not function properly, but with them it will stay healthy and be able to ward off diseases. Let me be clear. It is not what you eat or the pills that you take, but the beliefs about what you eat and the pills that you take that changes your body. It is not the eight glasses of water that keeps your body properly hydrated, but the belief that eight glasses per day are necessary. It is not the allergy shots that keep you allergy free, but the beliefs you hold about the shots. If you believe working out will keep your body tuned, it will. It is not cigarette smoke that kills you, but the power of what it is you believe about smoking. You have to believe something, as beliefs feed perception and it is your perception that creates your outer reality.

There are other fears that are based on beliefs, not about the body, but on how you are perceived by others. I recall that while I was still alive, as you understand it, seeing Walmart shoppers in various renditions of clothing that looked like they were dressed by a schizophrenic on an LSD trip. I could not understand how any of them could leave their house dressed as they were. What I know now is that they could care less about how others might perceive them. I felt the same way about a morbidly obese woman showing up at the beach in a bikini. I felt the same about a morbidly obese male showing up in a Speedo. What I didn't realize then was that they were more accepting of themselves than I was of my self. Rather than accept them I judged them. You all do it. Well, not all, but most. Some of you dress because you prefer how you look to yourself, while others dress to please or to not be judged by others, even though the clothes you are wearing are uncomfortable. So, if you dress the way you do simply because you like how you look, carry on. If you dress the way you do out of fear that others may judge you if you don't then you may want to reconsider your choice. The fear of being judged drives many of your beliefs. The fear of looking stupid is another. How many of you look around after tripping on a crack in the sidewalk? Treat that stumble as a lesson in self-acceptance.

When fear removes you from the present it shifts your attention into an undesirable future that does not exist...yet. Remember, you draw to you what you believe. Another fear is the fear of not being accepted, a belief based on your assumption that you are not worthy of being accepted just the way you are. Do not allow others to define you. Live your life as you desire and not on what you think others desire. This includes family and friends. If they are disappointed in you that is a judgment and a rejection, and says that they think they know better than you how you should live your life. You will feel that judgment. It is built into you. When you experience a rejection in your experience it is you rejecting yourself. Do you not approach someone out of fear of rejection?

How do You Identify What it is You Believe?

What you think you believe is not necessarily what you actually believe. Some of the time it is, like when you hear the rattle of that snake and you keep your distance. You believe that a rattlesnake is dangerous. It is a truth and a fact for you AND most people. You may believe that vaccinations are more dangerous than the illness it is designed to protect you from, while at the same time believing that the illness, let's say the flu, is something you 'catch.' Both are beliefs, of course, and with this combination of beliefs you have no protection at all. The power of vaccinations lies not in the concoction injected into your arm, but in the strength of the belief with which you infuse it. Another belief associated with whether you get the flu or not, and they are numerous, is that you do not choose the flu. You are a victim of it. In rejecting the vaccine, you couple that choice that says your own immune system is not stronger than the virus that 'attacks' you. Your immune system accommodates that belief.

You understand that you have chosen to refuse the vaccination, but you do not believe you have chosen to get the flu. That part of you that chooses does not judge good or bad. Getting the flu was

The Horse Rode Me

nothing more than bad luck to you. If you are an older person you believe that you are more prone to catching the flu and will have less chance of surviving it, and so the stronger that belief is the greater the chance of experiencing both. I can't impress upon you too much that beliefs drive your reality. If you strongly believe that vaccines will protect you then the greater the chance that they will. It has nothing to do with the power of the vaccine itself. It is the same with everything you experience. It is not the heroin or the alcohol that gets you hooked, but the intensity of the beliefs you have about them. They become facts of life. Remember the guru who ingested several tabs of LSD and his lack of reaction that changed Richard Alpert into Ram Dass.

What you experience in the moment will tell you what it is you believe. Your reality reflects back to you a symbolic representation of what it is you believe. Here's a big shocker: The outer world of form and substance is a symbolic representation of a literal inner world that you project outward. If you are good at interpreting your dreams then you will be good at interpreting your daily life. It is important to learn your own symbols. A dog to you may represent, friendliness, love and trust. Another person may see a dog as dangerous and to be approached, if at all, cautiously. The belief of person number two will make it more likely that he will be bitten by a dog. Because everything is connected, the outer world confirms for you what it is you believe. Before the age of 44 my father was allergic to pollen, cats and dogs. He slowly began changing his beliefs surrounding allergies as he realized he was creating his own allergies. As I told the story previously, he one day walked into the woods, hugged a tree, and replaced his old limiting belief with a new one. His allergies left him in that moment although he had been working on it for some time.

You can't change a belief simply by thinking it. For instance, if you jump off the Empire State Building and on the way down believe you'll land on your feet unscathed, you'll be shaking hands with me in no time. Thinking does not create a belief. Experience is what removes it from your tool box, and as I said before, you come with a few foundational beliefs to get you started. Whether you are an addict or not you are not going to 'think' yourself into a new belief. The first step is to accept the belief you currently hold, as in "I believe I am an addict and I accept that without judgment." Don't struggle against it, but as you take steps to loosen its grip you will find the struggle loses its intensity. For now, get yourself into rehab, and once clean start working on some of the things you're learning here. You also believe you will 'catch' Hepatitis C from sharing needles. The belief makes itself real. For you, your reality is real even though it is a play. You have forgotten you are an actor in your own creation.

The Horse Rode Me

The Horse Rode Me

It's Time to Disengage Your Auto-Pilot

Imagine yourself as the Captain of a sea going vessel, but you have no crew. Your ship is outfitted with an autopilot and weather radar. For the auto pilot to function it must be given a destination and in your case it's whatever it is you have chosen to explore this particular life you are currently living. For me the destination would be the land of the unusual. Of course, your ship is not heading for any geographical location, but rather a life direction. Sometimes it is a long trip of a hundred years and other times what it is you want to explore ends during your mother's first trimester. And yes, a fetus also chooses.

When you are fully present in the Now the auto pilot is disengaged and you are at the helm. Your physical senses are fully engaged. You smell and hear the bacon sizzling in the frying pan. You feel the frying pan handle in your hand and your feet solidly supporting you. Your mouth begins to water in anticipation of the taste that is soon to come. Your mind is at rest and neutral, simply bathing in the only moment that is actually real. But then something happens. Your mind leaves the present and you begin to worry about a past due bill. Your Monkey mind hates the Now. You imagine the worst result of an unpaid bill. Immediately your attention moves away from the Now and your autopilot engages. Your autopilot can only steer toward your destination and is not connected to your weather radar, nor can it see what is in front of it. It heads straight for a log that is in its path. You can't see it

The Horse Rode Me

because your attention is no longer present. Your ship hits the log which punches a hole in your bow. This shifts your attention back to the present where you notice your bacon is burned to a crisp. The burnt bacon was your choice because the you that chose it was on auto pilot at the time. Full consciousness was not given enough attention to remove the bacon before it burned.

Metaphorically this is what happens when your attention is not present, and let me assure you it happens to you all the time. Herein lies the futility of worry and guilt that I spoke of earlier. You are not well practiced at being present, which is your only point of power. When you are on autopilot you also cannot see your weather radar and often head straight for a storm. My storm was addiction. Had I been present my entire life I would have avoided the log and steered around the storm. I would have crossed the street directly rather than circling the globe to get to the other side. Attention is critical, and attention is not your thinking. Attention is who you are. Descartes' said, "I think therefore I am." NO! Your ATTENTION is who you are.

Your attention too often goes to your thinking, as in the example I gave of frying your bacon and then shifting your attention to your thinking and about the bill that was past due. You let the Monkey Mind steal you away from your own present moment. I was quite good a letting the Monkey Mind steer my ship. It became my autopilot gone crazy. It overwhelmed me with anxiety to the point of vomiting. I couldn't run a race in middle school without throwing up in the middle of the race. The Monkey Mind filled me with fear of not being good enough, a terrible feeling to live with and one I self-medicated with Xanax and heroin before I got clean. You are fully capable of shifting your attention off of your Monkey Mind and back to what is real in your present moment. Again, and this is critical, your thinking is not who you are. Your attention is who you are. You cannot know what belief is operative in the moment if **you** are not in the moment. You cannot determine what you are telling yourself in each moment if your attention is always on your thinking.

The Horse Rode Me

Thought

Thought is not consciousness. It is a tool **OF** consciousness, and as a tool it has a specific function. You believe thought initiates action when in reality its function is to interpret the reality you have created anew in each and every moment. You have gone so far as to believe that thinking **Is** consciousness. Thinking as mind is a trap. It is like using a screwdriver to loosen a nut. You may be able to loosen the nut sometimes, as when the nut is not too tight, but most of the time you won't budge it. Thought is a screwdriver for a screw, a wrench for a nut, a hammer for a nail. It is the interpreter of all the information/communications you continuously feed yourself. If your attention is always on your thinking it will not be able to do its job, for you are not feeding it any information. You employ thought as if was a communication in and of itself. If you are constantly engaging your thinking by directing your attention (you the chooser) to it then you give it no information to interpret.

'<u>Why</u>' did I do what I didn't want to do is the wrong question. Your information to Self lies in What you did. The 'what' carries all the information thought is programmed to interpret. What you do reflects the beliefs that feeds your perception, which in turn projects your outer reality. Keep in mind your outer world of things and substance is symbolic of your literal subjective inner world. You have it backwards and have for eons. Let's say you have an inner desire to pamper yourself. Thought may translate that into a want for pistachio ice cream. You then hop in your car and make a trip to your local grocery store for pistachio ice cream. Your literal inner world felt a desire to pamper yourself. Thought could have interpreted that in many ways, and all of them representative of a desire to pamper. Maybe you stopped washing your floor, grabbed your favorite book and reclined on your sofa to read it. Or maybe you ran a hot bubble bath. Or maybe you headed downtown for a manicure. The symbolic manifestation for pampering yourself could have taken numberless forms to represent the literal desire to pamper yourself. The inner is literal. The outer is symbolic and can take numberless forms.

Your wants are always the objective interpretation by thought of an inner subjective desire. If you are not paying attention to what you are doing then thought will often misinterpret your inner desire. When thought translates correctly we do what we want to do, and it only appears that thought is directing the action. Going to get ice cream when you want to be pampered is an example. When you spend much of your time obsessing and thinking, meaning your attention is focused on the Monkey Mind, then thought has little to interpret. The Monkey Mind spends much of its time in the past and in the future. Your thinking tells you that you want to cross the street to get to Starbucks. Half way across a car clips you and down you go. The way you see it is that you chose to cross the street, but you surely did not choose to be hit by that car. There are no accidents. As you were crossing the street your Monkey Mind went into hyper drive. Your girlfriend broke up with you. You were fired from your meaningless job. You were thinking what assholes people are and that you have the worst luck in the world. In that moment you were hit by the car, which confirmed everything you believed. You gave yourself proof of exactly what you believed in that moment.

The Horse Rode Me

Let's say you've finished my book and have begun to process and work the information. You decide to go for a relaxing drive along a scenic country road. It's Fall and the leaves have turned to brilliant reds and yellows and purples. The sun is out and you're at peace as you start your car's engine. You begin your drive and head for the perfect road. The traffic is light and you're cruising at a comfortable 45MPH. You come up quickly on a 2003 cream colored Chevy Impala (sorry dad) and you slow to 25MPH, an annoying speed for you. Annoyance is your first signal that there is a communication awaiting your attention. You notice the signal, but give it no further attention, hoping the old man (sorry dad) will soon turn off the road. Three miles later he's still in front of you oblivious, or so it seems to you, that you are even behind him. On this winding and hilly country road there is nowhere to pass. You notice that you are now frustrated, a stronger emotional signal. Two miles later you are still behind him and now you are really pissed. It's called anger, and when you experience this emotional signal you can see no choices to resolve your state of being. You have fallen back into pre The Horse Rode Me cause and effect behavior and thinking. You have paid no attention to your signals. You may have asked yourself the 'why' question, but as I have told you, that is the wrong question. What is happening in the moment you received the signal called annoying? The three signals, annoyance, frustration and anger were telling you that you shifted your attention from yourself and onto the old man driving the car in front of you. The 'why' analyses. The 'what' listens. 'What' provides thought enough information to translate what you are showing/telling yourself. If, at the annoyance signal, you turned your attention back to yourself and began enjoying the scenery again, you would have found the old man turning at the next aside street.

The belief system of good/bad, better/worse plays heavily in engaging your autopilot. Consider this scenario and how your beliefs flying around good/bad influence what and how you process your experience. You consider yourself a good person and it gives you pleasure helping others. For you, helping others is good, which is also a judgment. A friend calls and asks for your help in moving out of their apartment and into a new home they bought. You are happy to help even though you know that moving is a royal pain. Your whole day is spent lifting, hauling, unpacking and arranging. The day ends and you say your goodbye, but are not responded to with a big thank you. Now, even though you helped because helping makes you feel good you also had a belief that appreciation of that help should always be offered. You didn't get one and as you get in your car your first feeling is hurt. You would always thank a person for the help given you and because it is a guideline of yours you expect it from others. You then start asking the 'why' question and when you do that you go into analyzing, not you, but the other. They are rude. They don't appreciate the help you gave. They weren't brought up right. They're low class. Your Monkey Mind creates all kinds of reasons why they didn't thank you because you have a strong belief that thanking someone for a good they do is good and not thanking is bad.

You went immediately into judgment, which is a lack of acceptance. You required them to follow your guideline. You never get to that place of acceptance because you are hurt and your attention is now fully on your friend and on your thinking. You don't get to that understanding that you can only create your own reality. You do not create your friend's lack of verbal appreciation, but you do create your emotional response to that lack. It was your own belief that made you feel hurt and then it was your Monkey Mind that created all the negative scenarios that could have been the cause. So, if helping brings you pleasure, then help. If you believe that showing appreciation for help given then appreciate those that help you. It is not a cosmic rule that appreciation must be expressed verbally. If you find that this happens to you all too often you may want to consider that YOU create your own experience. Your judgment will draw to you that which you judge. You don't have to like it, but you do have to accept it. Drop the judgment. A week later a vase of roses arrives at your home with a thank-you note from your friend.

Overriding a Communication

Too much thinking (shifting your attention to your thinking) often overrides an emotional communication. Keep in mind that the feeling is a signal that you are receiving a communication. Let's say that you are a shy woman. You're at a restaurant having dinner by yourself. You look to your left and you see a handsome man eating alone. You catch his eye and you both turn away. You consider, but only for a second, asking him to join you. You feel an attraction, which holds a communication from your subjective (inner) self that you ignore because your Monkey Mind (thinking) kicks into high gear. Such a good-looking man would never be interested in joining me. He probably already has a girlfriend. With my luck he's probably gay and wouldn't be interested anyway. In those few thoughts you have engaged fear, a lack of self-acceptance and a lack of trust in your ability to create what you want. Your thinking overrides your attraction and desire, and replaces it with self-rejection.

Eliminating a Communication

There are certain situations when thought tells you that what you are feeling is inappropriate. Here again the belief system of good/bad joins the party. You're at work and you hear your boss groaning in the office next to yours. You leave your office to investigate and find your boss on the floor in pain. He is passing a kidney stone. You have worked for him for three years and can't remember a day when he hasn't been a real prick. Your initial feeling is one of pleasure. Karma, you think. He is getting what he deserves. Your thinking immediately engages at the onset of the feeling. It reminds you of the Sermon on the Mount. It tells you that you are a bad person for feeling pleasure at the pain of another. Under this barrage of the Monkey Mind you eliminate the initial feeling of pleasure and replace it with remorse. You were unaccepting of the initial feeling of pleasure and unaccepting of your self for having it. In the inappropriate use of thought the feeling of pleasure turned into its near opposite, guilt and self-deprecation.

The Camouflage of Positive Thinking

When you were a child your parents may have read to you The Little Engine That Could. It was first published in 1930. In the fairy tale the little engine encountered a mountain in which he had to pull several train cars. At first, he didn't think he could do it, but quickly changed to "I think I can. I think I can." As the little engine approached the top his thinking changed to, "I know I can. I know I can." It was my first remembered example of my thinking function morphing from doubt to possibility to assurance. It sounds like good advice for children, right? I thought so until the day I transitioned out of physical life. The problem as I now understand it is that thinking does not create your reality. It interprets it. Belief without any doubt is what creates the experience you want. When you reach that level of trust (without doubt) your actions will be automatic.

For instance, it takes no conscious effort to walk across the street. One step automatically follows the previous step, one after the other, until you step upon the curb on the other side of the street. You didn't have to think about moving every leg muscle to get your leg to move. In fact, doing that actually makes walking more difficult. So, what is the camouflage of positive thinking? The motivation for positive thinking is the fact that you do not believe, without any doubt, that you can do what you want to do. The closer you get to the 'without doubt' stage the more automatic doing what you want to do becomes.

For me, doing a 150lb clean and jerk was automatic. I had no doubt and believed fully (trusted) that I would get that bar over my head. As I put more and more weight on the bar my trust began to wane and my belief in limits kicked in. I could not think my way to a PR (personal record) although at the time I believed I could. PR's came slowly and with a lot of work. THIS is what I believed. They were never automatic, but as my belief in my ability to do it grew stronger based on my beliefs about hard work paying off, I was able to advance my lifting PR's. Once you start walking you no longer need to think about it, unless you suffer a spinal injury.

The Horse Rode Me

Then, your belief in your ability to walk goes from automatic to zero. The gorilla in the cage of positive thinking is that it is initiated by various levels of doubt and the erroneous belief that thinking creates.

You can visualize and think positively about an outcome until the end of time, but if the underlying beliefs are oppositional then you will not create what it is you want. One of the mottos of AA is, "One day at a time." It works because you don't have to think about the rest of your life, which doesn't exist anyway. All you have is the present moment. "One day at a time" or even better, one moment at a time has the ability to move your belief in recovery from zero to eight and eventually even to absolute. You WILL get to the point that you got to shortly after you began walking for the first time. Crawling was still easier but it severely limited your movement. You pushed forward until you no longer had to think about walking. Believe this: You WILL get to that point where sobriety becomes automatic just as walking did. AA needs to drop their opening greeting, "Hi, I'm David and I'm an addict." If you're not using you are not an addict. You'll never crawl again. It is only your thinking Monkey Mind that keeps you locked into that belief and it makes relapse so much easier.

Keep this rule in mind. Beliefs feed perception which then projects the outer image (the screen) you view as reality. Thought is a tool designed to watch the screen and interpret the outer symbolic image into a meaningful and literal inner communication. If your life sucks then it is to your beliefs that you must turn
Changing the Strength of a Belief

Your beliefs are well fed, especially those that have garnered full trust and have gone to autopilot. They are as well muscled as I was before leaving you and will not be easily pushed aside. What you actually do in the moment will reveal to you the operative belief in the moment. Some are stronger than others. You've seen demonstrations of hypnosis before, and at some level have marveled at the power of an implanted belief. But you never took it any farther than that. It's time you did. You also think that your concentration is piloted by your thinking. No, what you are <u>doing</u> reveals what you are actually concentrating on.

You have probably noticed that when someone challenges you on something you feel strongly about that you dig in your heels, especially if they call you names. The same thing happens with beliefs. You cannot oppose them without strengthening them. Beliefs become more compliant to change when they are accepted. In the deepest sense beliefs are neutral. Anthony Hopkins doesn't judge Hannibal Lecter's murderous ways, for Hannibal IS Anthony. Split Jeans did not judge my addiction, for Split Jeans is me, and Soul does not judge you, for you are Soul. In that same way you must first accept/not judge the belief you are trying to replace. It is merely a choice. You draw to you that which you oppose with judgment. If you believe the world is full of comatose drivers you will see them everywhere, thus confirming the belief. The more you oppose your belief in the addictive power of heroin the more addictive it will become.

Numerous beliefs intertwine themselves with addiction. Most of which are self-defeating, and some of them I mentioned earlier. For one hour during your day write down what you are doing, not what you are thinking, although you will often shift your attention to your thinking. Then, next to what you do, write down the belief behind the doing. Here are some examples. At 1:15 pm you get into your car and begin driving to your dealer. The motivation is the belief that you need a fix. Your body is responding to your beliefs regarding how long you can go between fixes. Behind the actual need is the belief that you will get dope sick if you don't get a fix soon. You drive within the speed limit. The belief is that with your luck you'd get stopped for speeding. Part of this is your Monkey Mind talking to you about luck and police. During that moment your attention is split between the driving and your thinking. You reach the parking lot of the local mall where your dealer agreed to meet you. He's not there yet and this is where your Monkey Mind really kicks in gear. You don't notice that the sun is

The Horse Rode Me

shining and that you are parking under a maple tree that provides some shade. As long as your attention is focused on your thinking you are giving thought nothing to interpret.

You check your mirrors for police. You believe they are always on the lookout for heroin addicts. A cruiser pulls behind you and you see the cop on his radio. He's checking your plates, but you know everything is up to date. Your Monkey Mind is telling you that you should have parked among all the other cars, but your idiot dealer told you to meet him under the only maple tree in the lot. To you, you are a strobe light in a dark room. You check your wallet making sure you have the right amount for five bags. Again, this is in response to your thinking mind. You have not noticed the music from your car radio nor the sunshine or the shade. With relief you notice the cop driving away. The belief is no cops is a good thing. The emotional signal was relief. Thus far you have been in a state of perpetual anxiety and have given thought virtually nothing to interpret. You have been living in a fear filled future by way of your anxiety. Maybe you get the point. When you are an addict rarely do you exist in the moment without fear.

Don't give up. Changing beliefs is no easy thing. Getting 275lbs over my head would never have happened if I went from 175lbs directly to 275. Be smart. Take a break. Do something fun, but always come back to changing the beliefs that do not serve you. Look first to what you hold as a fact, for they are the strongest of your beliefs. You may want to practice first on the weaker beliefs. Here are a few easier beliefs that you can first accept and then gradually insert a replacement like... I have to put on make-up to look beautiful. No, you don't. I have to brush my teeth up and down to get them clean. No, you don't. I have to drink eight glasses of water every day to stay hydrated. No, you don't. I need a new car to be looked up to. No, you don't. If my friends are drinking, I need to drink too. No, you don't. It's rude not to accept a hit of weed passed to me. No, it's not. My lawn can't have weeds. Yes, it can. I need supplements to make my body strong. Only if you believe you do. I can't. Yes, you can. Remember, you are connected to everything and everything longs to give you what you believe. If you believe you are worthless, let me tell you this. You have literally participated in every event, large and small, good and bad, that has happened on your planet from the moment you were born. You hold the power over you and that power lies in what you believe.

The Horse Rode Me

The Power of Perception

If I haven't blown your mind yet you better get ready. What I have laid out for you thus far will ultimately become the groundwork for a totally new psychology based on who you really are and not who you think you are. You have been an eagle that thinks he is a snake. It is now time to wake up and fly. Each of you, by way of your perception, creates matter. Matter does not exist without your perception of it. Consciousness does not arise out of matter. Matter arises out of consciousness. Your perception is an actual mechanism that is not a part of your body and resides outside of it. Recall that I told you earlier that the brain is a conduit for consciousness and does not generate it. Perception is a mechanism of consciousness similar to your ear being a mechanism for hearing. Perception creates matter. You currently believe that perception 'takes in' a pre-existing solid reality, when the reality is that perception projects out and then your senses receive the reflection of what you have projected outward... created. I've touched on perception being the projector and beliefs being the film. Perception creates matter. I cannot stress that enough, for when you finally get it, everything will change for you. Without perception there is no matter. Nothing your senses pick up exists without your creation of it. Nothing material preexists your perception.

Your five senses, sight, hearing, taste, smell and touch, are receiving mechanisms of what you have created outwardly in each and every moment. They allow you to experience that which you have created. What you create is a symbolic representation of what you are experiencing literally through your inner subjective self. The projection of your perception arises simultaneously with your inner subjective state. It is immediate. As I said before, the inner is literal and the outer is symbolic. It is no wonder that you are as screwed up as you are when you have the whole thing ass backwards. You create the form of everything, but not the energy of the form. How many outer projections can you create to reflect sadness? How many for happiness? The outer is thus limitless while the inner is singular. You are all highly imaginative in your creations. As an example, you can create limitless outer manifestations to represent happiness, just as you can for sadness. Go for happiness.

You also do not understand imagination. It is the seat of creativity and therefore a part of perception. Imagination is as real as the apple you bite. Consequences, inspiration, accomplishments, and failure arise in your outer world by way of your imagination and the projection of your perception. What you imagine you will eventually translate into reality. If you imagine you are lower than pond scum you will meet with the proof that you are. If you can imagine yourself to be sober, healthy, prosperous and happy then your perception will do all it can to make it happen, and so will the rest of the world that surrounds you. Beware, however, of conflicting beliefs, as beliefs feed your perception.

I also mentioned the importance of attention earlier. It also provides input to perception. While you are reading my book, your perception is creating the book, the chair that you sit in, the room that holds you, as well as everything outside your window when you look up from the book. You all do this and it happens instantly. You are all magical. Every moment of your life is more magical than your highest dope high. Throughout your human history you have been doing this, but you are now waking up. You are slowly realizing that what you have been taught about yourself and your reality is no longer serving you. You have explored everything you can by forgetting who you are. It is you that has chosen to awaken, and you are awakening to the illusion that you are all separate. The heroin epidemic, as I said, is the symbol you have created to reflect to yourselves the destructive nature of your strong belief that you are separate. Addicts are the heroes and heroines of this symbol. You are connected to everything.

The Horse Rode Me

From the beginning of human time perception has created a reality of separateness. As you become more self-aware perception will reflect the new reality of connectedness. Perception has created the illusion of separateness, for that is what you have believed. It has created separate beings from you that you have been taught are lesser than you or greater than you, when all along the reality is that you are all One. Your belief that you are separate has served a purpose, but you can go no further with it. You are in the process of remembering who you are. You are remembering your own Split Jeans. Your senses reflect that everything is outside of you. The rock, the tree, the Sun, the toad, your girlfriend, your boyfriend all represent your belief that you are separate. As you become more aware you realize that it is your perception that creates the reality of separateness that you experience.

You are **NOT** separate from everything. Everything is a part of you and you are a part of everything. As you become more self-aware you approach the point where you can accept connectedness and the lack of separation without it threatening your individual identity. <u>Interconnectedness is not a threat to your individual identity!</u> You do not have to consciously know that you are interconnected for it to influence your perception. Keep in mind there is no official reality. <u>There is ONLY your reality</u>. If you don't like it, it is up to you to change it. You are right to ask how you all create such a similar outer world. The question comes from your deep belief that you are all separate. Think of yourselves as a single organism where every aspect of the organism is in constant awareness of every other aspect of its self. Everything you do, whether it be physical or mental, ripples out and affects the whole. Think of the madness that would ensue if you and thousands of others sitting in a football stadium could not agree on what you are watching or even where you are. Your interconnectedness is responsible for the similarities you all create. All of them, however, are subtly different.

As you become more self-aware you may find that you have

The Horse Rode Me

been looking at your reality through a straw. You are limited only by what you believe about your reality. Any thing that has an objective awareness, which means having a physical reality, has perception. This means that you, cats, dogs, trees, anything physical projects by way of their perception its physical reality. Everything is conscious energy that your perception coalesces into matter. Without a physical orientation (meaning existing in any reality that involves matter) there is no need for perception. Where Split Jeans/Me now inhabit there is no need for perception as We/I are no longer physical. My father once told me that miracles don't go against reality. They go against what we believe about reality. He first read this in Jane Robert's book, The Nature of Personal Reality in 1985.

The Horse Rode Me

Changing Your Perception

You must relax to change your perception because you have held your current beliefs about it as truth. You're not going to change your rust bucket car into a Maserati by crossing your eyes and smoking a blunt. But, remember those Magic Eye posters? Looking straight at them allows you to see only the surface. If you defocus and try to see through it a 3D image pops out at you. You will be able to replace the straw-like view you currently have with an expansive more inclusive reflection of who you are and how you are connected to everything. Because you don't question your perception it takes a volitional willingness to expand it. Perception creates a world that is totally real to you in each and every moment. You <u>CAN</u> expand it.

In general, your perception will match that of the individual you are with. You will both see a hawk swooping down and snatch a squirrel out of a tree. Your reality has to be this way or you'd all feel like each other is crazy. However, in relation to how you process what you have experienced, how you express what it is you have experienced, what you believe about it and how you engage it does NOT always match that of the person you are with who <u>Basically</u> experienced the same thing. These differences are also mediated by your perception. In this sense there is nothing to argue about, as your perception is different than his/her perception. Both perceptions are true for each of you. You both see a blue sky and green grass but your experience of it is different.

There are times when your perception will create differently than the majority of other people. They may even convince you that what you perceived was wrong. Let's say ten people witnessed a crime committed by a felon wearing a leather jacket. Nine of the witnesses created the felon wearing a black jacket, but you perceived it as being blue. Generally, you will be swayed by the majority that you did not see the jacket correctly. This is how it would go under your current understanding of your reality. The Jacket and its color preexisted your perception of it rather than you each created the jacket in the moment. Nine created a black jacket while you created a blue jacket. You had to be wrong...right? The jacket couldn't be two colors at once. You never say, "for me the jacket was blue." When you believe the world of matter preexists your perception of it this is exactly how you react to being 'wrong.' In the not too distant future you will only wonder why you reconfigured the black jacket to be blue.

You will and have reconfigured the projected energy (in my example the felon). What you deal with is the energy projected to you whether it be a person, place or thing. That person, place and thing is pure energy that your perception changes into a thing your senses can detect. **You** are pure energy that another's perception configures as you for their senses to detect. If you are with ten people, each of them creates their version of you. Yes, there is your energy, but through knowing and appreciation you allow yourself to be configured as the 'other' sees fit. You are not alone and only dealing with your own energy. It is not just the physical form that is projected to you, but the emotional content as well. You run into trouble when you reconfigure the emotional content of another's projected energy. If you are angry and the other is calm you may, at times, configure their energy to match your own. You will find them quite surprised at your reaction to them. In the reverse you may think you are projecting a calm energy, but it is laced with anger under the surface and the other picks up on the anger. It is most important to be in tune with the energy you project.

You are always creating your solid reality through your perception, but you do not create any other sentient being's reality. How they project back to you is their choice. You cannot, nor have you ever, been able to choose for another, but you can be privy to another's reality by way of your interconnectedness. All of your individual realities are intertwined because you are all interconnected. You all influence each other because you are connected. By expanding your perception, you can begin to see more realities than your own. I know how much stress you carry. I have carried quite a load of it myself. The most effective way to control what your perception projects right in front of you is to stay in the present moment.

Here's an example of staying present and taking advantage of connectedness. Before typing these few paragraphs my father was in the woods cutting down a large dead oak tree. He figured the angle of the fall and began his cut. When 2/3 of the way through the tree began leaning 25 degrees away from where my father believed it would fall and the tree locked the saw bar into itself. His first thought was F..., what a pain in the ass. The feeling/signal was frustration, but he did not dwell on it. He knew he created the experience. No one was at fault, as there was actually only an experience. Not right, not wrong...neutral. He knew he needed another chain saw to fell the tree and loosen the tree's grip on his saw. He walked away from the tree, calm and present, and walked to a neighbor's house and borrowed their saw. Fifteen minutes later the tree fell exactly where he had originally felt it would fall and he easily removed his own saw. Where he originally thought the tree should fall was exactly where it did fall. He was not wrong and understood that his goal was met, but the process by which it was met was different than what he expected. This is a lesson also of trusting the goal, but allowing the process to unfold as it would, and not by way of your own expectations regarding the process.

The point about staying in the present moment is about noticing what is around you and that in the vast majority of instances, you are safe. You notice your feelings which are nothing more than signals and are meant to be as brief as a knock at the door. I remind you that a lingering feeling is your warning bell that you are no longer present and that you have shifted your attention to your thinking that has probably moved either to the past or to the future. Feelings are important to perception, but only as signals and as such hold no more importance than traffic lights. The importance of traffic lights lay in what each colored light conveys. Like traffic lights your feelings covey a message that is being conveyed. They are not the message itself. You have been trained to focus on the feeling and therefore provide no further information for thought to interpret. If you focused as much on the color of a traffic light and ignored what the light conveyed, you'd go deaf from the car horns blaring at you. You do this with your feelings because long ago you somehow learned to believe that the feeling was the message itself. Things went to hell in a hand basket ever since.

In focusing on the feeling, you allow IT to tell you what to do. You stop paying attention to you and focus on what you believe to be the cause of your feeling. I did it all the time. If someone pissed me off, whether it was a friend or a stranger, I never said to myself, "what is this trying to tell me about me." Typically, I'd let them know what I felt about them. Sometimes I'd stop seeing them for a while if they were my friend. The point is, I always responded as if the feeling was the communication itself, which completely takes my attention off of me and onto who or what I believed to be the 'cause' of my feeling. I hope you're getting the idea I pointed out early in my book that you are playing baseball on a basketball court using a golf club as a bat. Your feelings are never created by other persons, places or things. They are created by you, just as the scene was created by you.

So, your perception instantly created the outer symbolic scene to send you a message that your inner literal self wanted to convey. It is not about the other person or the scene. Getting sucker punched in a bar puts you into a rage...if you're not knocked out. You drew the energy of the individual that punched you. Your perception configured that energy into the guy that hit you. His hitting you and you getting hit were a mutual agreement of choices in that moment, just like Anthony Hopkins acting a scene with Jodi Foster. In this example you created an experience that was oppositional to yourself. Most, if not all, of your negative feelings puts you into blame mode, while you often attribute your positive feelings to someone else initiating them. Blame is a chocking vine that squeezes the life out of you. Recognize it and cut it out at the roots, for it is the motivator of vengeance, vindictiveness, justification and ultimately war. These are as much a waste of energy as are guilt and worry. Blaming is like a thief in the night stealing your home's electric generator during a storm blackout.

Comfort, fun and happiness are far more available to you than you realize and the key is being present and shutting down your Monkey Mind that loves living in the past and the future...and blaming. And to do so the Monkey Mind must lie to you. Do not allow your feelings motivate you. They are signals, not communications. Directing your reality are no more the function of feelings than a golf club hitting a baseball. Letting your feelings direct your actions is what keeps you from comfort, fun and happiness. You create it all. You are connected to it all, and you can change it all. Perception is your tool for changing to the life you want, and the life an addict wants is a sober life. What you think and feel does not create your life, but it does influence your perception, which DOES create your life. Where your attention goes will change your perception. Look around you and stop directing your attention to your thinking.

Remember also that in addition to creating your own reality and then reflecting what you created back to you, you also act as a mirror for whoever you are interacting with. You are the energy they solidify into you as the reflection their senses interpret. This is how interconnectedness works. You are all reflecting back to yourselves and mirroring for others. By being present and opening your awareness you will also be better able to understand what the person you are using as a reflection is getting from you as his mirror. You can know this were it not for what it is you EXPECT to see in the 'other.' Perception creates based not only on the beliefs you feed it, but the expectations those beliefs create.

The Horse Rode Me

Perception, Light and Time

It is difficult for you to imagine your reality without light and time. Time creates the illusion for you that every moment is connected to the next moment. You understand time as linear. A cancer found early allows enough 'time' for a cure to be enacted. This is what you believe and that is what your perception projects outward. It never occurs to you that your life is similar to a roll of film where each frame is a still life photo of each and every moment of your life. It is only your beliefs that keep you from curing your cancer from one frame to the next. It is your beliefs that keep you addicted. It is the combination of light and time that allows for your perception to create matter. It is the incredibly slow movement of time that allows for your creation of matter. Time is bent in your reality. In realities that do not have matter time moves at such an incredibly fast speed that it is virtually simultaneous. Think of it this way: Imagine yourself at the precipice of a black hole just before you got sucked in and disappeared into nothingness. At this point of the precipice of the densest gravity in the Universe, you turn to your left and see the entire history of planet earth in less time than the single beat of a hummingbird wing. Imagine an eternal being on your planet from its birth looking up at that black hole. For the entire life of the planet this eternal being would see you never move from the spot he saw you first over four billion years ago. If you don't believe me, ask an astro physicist. Gravity affects time.

   I tell you this to try and impress upon you that you live in a reality far stranger than you have imagined. Yours is not the only reality in which you play and explore. If you can imagine the possibility that what I am saying is true don't you think God could as well? Light is also needed in your reality to give depth to what you create. Without light there can be no matter, no 'you' as you know yourself to be. Now, here's a kicker about light. If you had no perception you would not be able to generate light. Perception creates the objects that generate light...light bulbs, fires, stars. You believe that light is generated by these things/bodies, but it is you that create these things/bodies. You create them through your perception and the slow speed of time in your reality. PERCEPTION CREATES LIGHT.

   I know that you have never imagined what I am telling you in this book while you were whacked on heroin, maybe on LSD, but not on heroin. You may have caught a glimpse of it on an acid trip, as did Ram Das, but that pales in comparison to what you do every moment of your life. Look around you. Everything you see, hear, smell, taste and feel you create through the projection of your perception. If you could see what it is your perception turns into matter you would never again doubt that you are connected to a kaleidoscopic whole of a swirling, wondrously colorful, montage of conscious energy. Your individuality is a microscopic eddy in the whole of that montage. Start believing it now. Your life will change. I know many of you have never felt like you fit in…the proverbial square and triangular pegs trying to squeeze into a round hole. Here's why.

The Horse Rode Me

The Agreement You Made Before Coming Here

There is but one agreement you must make before coming to your current playing field, and it has nothing to do with gender. It has everything to do with how you will perceive and process what it is you create. There are three perceptual filters through which you process the information of your world. You must agree to experience at least three lives on earth, one for each perceptual filter. In terms of sexual orientation, male and female is an agreed upon element of your reality. It is in place when you come into your body. Its sole purpose is to allow entrance into your world as a physical being. You can experience your world three times as the same gender as long as you fulfill your obligation to experience the three perceptual filters. Everything else regarding gender is a belief, some of which are so strong they are held as a truth and are therefore never questioned. Every culture holds different beliefs about gender, as you well know. Unfortunately, most of them denigrate women. There is only one agreed upon truth about gender and it is that there is male and female. Everything else is belief based. That women are weaker and more emotional than men are a belief and not a truth. Although if you believe this strongly enough it is a truth for you.

You have become quite confused about sexuality because you think only in terms of gender, although you have now included homosexual, bisexual and transgender into the mix. This, however, has nothing to do with the three filter sets you have agreed to experience. I am calling the three perceptual filters round, square and triangle, even though others have called them common, intermediate and soft. Male, female, homosexual, bisexual and transgender can have any of the three perceptual filters. As an example, a set of identical male triplets will seem very different to others if each of them has a different perceptual filter. Two of them

The Horse Rode Me

will try to fit in, while the round will feel at home within his culture. He may, however, think his brothers are a bit odd. A full sixty-six percent of humans have the round perceptual filter and so it is the rounds that set the rules that the squares and triangles feel obliged to abide by. Squares and triangles feel like outsiders as they grow up because they see the world differently than the majority rounds.

Many squares and triangles, feeling out of place and more disconnected than most, try to fit in, and in the trying they never feel right. As I said before, you can't squeeze a square or triangle into a round. You are already bad at accepting differences, but you are improving. If you have felt different all of your lives then you are probably either a square or a triangle. You never feel right unless you never fell into the trap of trying to fit in. The combinations are these: male round, square and triangle, and female round square and triangle. The three that you must fulfill under your agreement are round, square and triangle. All three can be done in one gender. You could have 5,000 lives and all but two of them could be round as long as one was square and one was triangle. I have had 2,784 lives. Some have had three. Old souls are not really old, since all time is simultaneous. Old souls are those who have had many many lives on Earth.

The preponderance of addicts are squares and triangles. They are most often the ones that feel so disconnected by way of not feeling they fit in, not realizing that they not only perceive the world differently than the majority rounds, but also process their experiences differently. It is no wonder that many of them turn to drugs when their beliefs and the rounds see them as more disconnected then the rounds see themselves. The truth that I keep reminding you of is that you are all magnificently interconnected. Think of how disconnected a born-again Christian homosexual male or female must feel who also happens to be square or triangle. My best friend, Michael, who was neither born again nor homosexual, was a triangle. He felt very alone despite the continuous love and support he received from his family. Michael was a soldier of the symbol and pre-deceased me by way of a heroin overdose. And, like me, he is not dead. He's just not there with you.

Rounds comprise 66% of you, squares 21% and triangles 13%. No matter which perceptual filter you choose before coming into your current form you cannot change once here. Each of the three, however, can influence each other, but cannot become one of the other two. If you are round, you will recognize those who are square and triangle. Triangles take the most heat because they are the least represented in the global population. They take the heat because you are bad at acceptance. Being different is not a dirty word. Each and every one of you is the normal you. Used in any other sense you should consider assigning the word 'normal' to the trash heap of history. Millions of people would still be alive.

The Horse Rode Me

Exploring the Perceptual Filters

Round
This majority filter is the most rational, and the one that creates your mass beliefs. They are drawn to the physical world and draw their information and communications from it. This is typically what you assign to the male gender in your western culture. Rounds are most fascinated by things outside of themselves. They trust what they see, feel, taste, touch and hear. Rounds are most interested in what their perception projects outwardly. Art, technology and mechanics draw the rounds. Because you assign these interests generally to the male gender, historically you have looked upon female rounds with some suspicion, as if they are not true to their gender. They are true to their perceptual filter, but are somewhat repressed by their cultural beliefs. Keep in mind that in your reality gender only refers to your role in the perpetuation of the species. Because you assign cultural limits on gender you thwart both genders from fully expressing their interests and motivations. For you males, 34% of you are squares and triangles. You do not process your information as do the rounds, and yet you also try to fit in not only by way of your perceptual filters, but to cultural gender roles as well. You have done this from the beginning of time.

Square
This filter focuses on interaction and involvement with all things in your reality, not just other people. Be it people, animals, nature, the universe, ideas and concepts, the squares will be interactive with them. The squares gather their information both subjectively (inward as do triangles) and objectively (outwards as do rounds.) They are passionate and flamboyant and will often be involved in causes and movements. Their own outer creations will draw their attention, but in general they are more attuned to their

subjective states. Since their primary focus is on interaction they are rarely found alone, as isolation is abhorrent to them. Isolation causes them great conflict as they process much of their communications through interactions. Squares, because their filter is that of interaction, are most attuned to the interconnectedness of all things.

Triangle
Triangles are the least prevalent of the three filter sets, and are the most inward looking. They connect best with other triangles and some squares since the square filter contains aspects of both rounds and triangles. They view and understand their world through the self first and so interactions can be frustrating with rounds in particular, for they each do not understand the other. They tend to hold themselves responsible for the actions of others and this includes all three filter groups. Triangles are the ones most prone to be saying 'sorry' no matter whether you see them at fault or not. In trying to accommodate their understanding of their reality to the rounds, triangles are often the most unhappy and frustrated of the three. Also, since their focus is so inwardly directed they have the greatest need for intimate relationships, but will meet with great difficulty if their partner is not also a triangle. Relying primarily on the inner sense of themselves and others they appear to be the most dependent. The outer world of matter and form means the least to them.

Why we need to know that the three perceptual filters exist
From the very beginning we are taught to act either male or female based on our physiology. Girls are given dolls and dressed in pink, while boys are given trucks and erector sets and dressed in blue. Girls are demure and emotional, while boys are aggressive and rational…or so you believe. These are nothing more than cultural beliefs that you foist upon your children. The majority of you believe the world that your child is born into pre-exists their entry into it. That is to say your little boy sees a toy truck that pre-exists his perception of it, and your little girls sees a little doll that pre-exists her perception of it. Few of you believe that your

children literally create the world in which they have come to romp in, or that there may be more than one way in which to perceive it. Two thirds of you give birth to a round, who 'fits in' pretty well in a world that his or her 'kind' dominates.

In identifying male or female we confuse gender with perception, or perceptual filters. Another individual may hold the same gender as you, but there is only a 2 in 3 chance if you are round that you are interacting with someone of the same perceptual filter. A triangle has only a 1 in 9 chance of interacting with someone of the same filter, and square has a 1 in 5 chance. We do tend, however, to draw those of the same perceptual filter to us. In relationships we get along best with a partner of the same filter, for our perception of ourselves and the world is similar. Since perception forms our world and we don't realize it, a square has difficulty understanding a round and a round has difficulty understanding a square. They literally see the world differently and this is compounded by our belief in one immutable reality that is merely perceived differently by each of us. This is true for all mixes of filter partnerships. Women are from Venus and men are from Mars is more a comment on cultural beliefs than on gender, and it is only accurate for round males and triangular females. Therefore, it makes for a lot of unhappy people, especially females, for only 13% of our population has the triangle filter. Because of mass beliefs, many triangle and square males try to squeeze themselves into a perceptual filter that is not theirs. Round and square females do the same thing.

In the west you are now beginning to see both men and women break out of the two gender stereotypes and begin sharing the two gender beliefs. Primarily, however, it is women moving into the majority perceptual filter set of round. You see women in sports, managing companies, carrying arms and occupying many more fields that are easily moved into by the rounds. You hear of men getting in touch with their feminine side, which is good for square and triangle men, but not good for round. The squares can do both. So, you are beginning to allow cross-over, but cross-over based solely on gender. We are asking 66% of men to give equal time to the triangle perception that is not theirs. Thirteen percent of men in the triangle perception are already from Venus and have been pressured by your belief systems all their lives to act as though they were round, and therefore from Mars. These men are definitely not from Mars. Finally, the 21% of men who are of the square perception are stuck between a rock and a hard place. The numbers are different for women. Sixty-six percent of women who are round are finally released from their bondage of trying to fit into the triangle way of seeing things. They can become who they always were. The 13% who are already triangle are given the luxury of remaining who they already are now that feminist militancy is dying down. The 21% of women who are of the square perception are stuck, like the men, between a rock and a hard place.

You move with greater ease in a relationship when the other individual has the same perceptual filter. This is independent of gender. Two round male homosexuals have a better chance at a lasting relationship than a heterosexual couple where one is round and the other is square. When different filters couple in a relationship their perceptions of reality will not be the same. Conflicts arise because one partner sees and creates the world one way and the other sees and creates it another way. Both feel their way is the right way, not realizing they are both correct. But, because you don't understand the three perceptual filters and try to squeeze all perception into two genders, conflicts arise. There are other reasons for conflict, but this is an important point. Every individual on this planet creates their own reality. There is no THE REALITY that is perceived differently by different people. You believe reality is out there to be perceived and so you argue your perception as being the correct perception, and in this you move into comparisons and have trouble accepting differences.

A woman who is a square and therefore flamboyant, involved and requiring interaction, will meet with confusion if she is married to a man who is a triangle. He processes the world inwardly through self first. He is not interested in involvement, interaction or mass movements as is his square wife. If they are both true to their own perception many arguments will arise, because both hold different perceptions and therefore different realities and don't realize it. If they both try to fit in to the round majority they will not understand why they are both unhappy all the time. They may be depressed and not know why. They are told it is a chemical problem in their brains and so both begin a regimen of anti-depressants. If the triangle male tries to squeeze himself into his square wife's perception, he will be unhappy and his wife will not understand why. With two genders and three perceptual sets, and with rounds (66%) creating your mass beliefs, it is no wonder there is so much conflict and misunderstanding in relationships. Even when square joins with square and triangle with triangle they will meet with some difficulties because they find themselves in a world where the belief systems are created by the rounds.

Since triangles process the world in an inward manner they are often at odds with society and the official reality generally created by the round orientation. Many triangles are introverts. They are agitated, restless and frustrated much of the time because when they try to create their reality according to the rules established by the rounds they find themselves unsatisfied. Even if their creations fit in beautifully they remain unsatisfied for it is not who they are and it is not how they naturally create. Of the three filter sets, the triangles compare themselves to others the most. My hope is that this information will liberate countless squares and triangles. The acceptance of three filter sets will require an overhaul of our current understanding of psychology.

All three perceptions will meet with frustration and conflict - less so with round - because of your officially accepted understanding of reality, which holds to two genders whose perceptual orientations are not supposed to cross gender. This is why a round female used to feel out of the loop before the women's movement, and is also why the women's movement doesn't quite hit the mark. There are too few boxes to fit everyone into. This is also why all women do not embrace the feminist movement. Triangles in particular may have been quite content the way things were, except for unequal pay for equal work. Each perceptual way of being has its own challenges.

Like attracts like, and in this sense each perception is attracted to the same perception. This creates greater ease within the relationship because each partner talks the same language, so-to-speak. In general, when two different perceptions come together the relationship is not likely to last because of the great energy required to make it work. That is not to say they cannot work and many have, but an understanding of this information will make such relationships easier.

A female triangle, because of her minority perceptual filter, may feel more at home in a <u>belief system</u> that allows her to more easily honor her way of seeing/processing the world. A male triangle will find great difficulty fitting into a round dominated world. Because of your beliefs surrounding gender you place male triangles and squares into the effeminate world and often suspect they are gay. You will often describe square and triangle males as being in touch with their feminine side, when the reality is they actually process the world differently than do you…if you are round. The same is done to females that hold the round filter. You place them into the masculine world. Think of how much freedom you deny yourselves because of your current beliefs surrounding gender alone. You are all responding to gender by way of your beliefs, and not by way of the reality by which you have designed your world.

Education is another way the rounds disadvantage the squares and triangles. Thirty four percent of the children of the world are being taught by a method that best suits the rounds. This further isolates 1/3 of the world's children. Think of how much the world loses when 1/3 of the population is taught in a way that does not match the way in which they process their information. Then add to that the belief that you are all separate from everything there is.

The Horse Rode Me

Squares and triangles comprise two billion people in a world of six billion. That's a boat load of people that often feel they have to 'fit in' in order to be accepted because they see themselves and are seen by the rounds as being so different. Think for a moment what it must have felt like for your homosexual brothers and sisters to have lived their true identities in a 'closet' before you gradually opened to their desire to 'come out.' Then add to that the concept of three perceptual filters, which puts one third of them in another closet. Most remain in this other closet and wonder why they still feel so different even after 'coming out.' They are doubly screwed because of your lack of acceptance. You do not allow people to be who they have chosen to be before they ever joined you in your world.

This problem runs even deeper when looking only at gender and the beliefs we attach to male/female. If you are a round male you feel most at home, but not completely. Consider a round male and his desire to be a ballet dancer. It is the same for you females. A round female auto mechanic is looked upon with suspicion. Not knowing who you are creates problems for all of you. Round males and females also try to fit in to your beliefs surrounding gender by suppressing their real interests so as not to be judged by their non-accepting peers. Fearing for their children, parents will steer them into interests that might create the least degree of unhappiness. Male rounds are rarely given the opportunity to play with dolls even though their intent in coming into your physical reality may be to explore nurturance, and so they must walk around the globe to get to the other side of the street. Add to this the deep feelings of separation and isolation that addicts feel, male and female. You might have an appreciation for the addicts' desire for a moment of false peace that heroin delivers. There are two billion alienated people by perceptual set alone. Add to this skin color, socio-economic status, your level of education, et.al, and you see the problem you have created for yourselves. Damn, you are more different by way of your perceptual filters than you are by the short list I just cited.

The Horse Rode Me

The Horse Rode Me

The Chicken or the Egg

What I have shared has given you the tools to create the life you want. You now have the baseball bat with which to hit the baseball, but in your reality, you have the choice to continue using the golf club if it is your desire to do so. Just know that if you continue to use the golf club, you will continue being a victim; continue with blaming others; continue thinking you create some experiences, but not all of your experience; continue believing in luck and accidents and meaningless coincidences; continue trying to fix a loved one <u>you</u> believe would be happier if they lived the life you think would be better for them, and continue believing miracles appear through the magic of God. Most importantly you will continue to believe you are connected to nothing except through your genes. Much of the magnificence of your reality and who you are I have not shared. There is so much more. What I will say, however, is that you have chosen one of the most challenging realities, and for that you are to be commended. You threw yourself into the most complex of playing fields that throughout your entire history you have played completely on auto-pilot. You have now chosen to wake up.

With these game rules I have shared with you, you may create many of the same scenarios that arise in conjunction with your feeling signals, but you will understand that it is you that created them. There is great power and freedom in knowing that, as well as great responsibility. If you strike out with the bat it is on you.

The Horse Rode Me

Striking out with the golf club makes it easy for you to blame the golf club. Think of your beliefs as the bat. If you're facing a fastball pitcher you might choose a lighter bat to get around on the pitch sooner. This would be akin to choosing a different belief. How much easier is it to change something in you than to change someone else, which you never can anyway? You provide yourself with no information about yourself when calling the driver that pulled out in front of you an asshole. Heroin will no longer hold the power any more than the pills you pop for your health hold the power. You will understand that heroin and your near limitless medications represent the power with which you have infused them by way of your beliefs. Remember Ram Das, the old Hindu guru and LSD. That old man did not have an LSD blocker hardwired into his brain.

The Monkey Mind will not loosen its vice-like grip on your beliefs without a fight. While reading this book I know that it had reared its insecure pinhead at every turn. But, that soft whisper you have ignored for so long also spoke to you. There is an aphorism you have all heard: The squeaky wheel gets the grease. My admonition is; do not grease the egoic Monkey Mind. Your ego is your tool designed to connect you to your physical world. The Monkey Mind is an aberration created by you out of fear and misunderstanding of who you are. For addicts that monkey has morphed into King Kong. Every time you go against one of your inner guidelines the monkey gains ten pounds. Under the influence of heroin you break those guidelines every minute of every day. You hurt others and you hurt yourselves. However, it does not change the core of who you are; that beautiful boy (or girl) my parents never lost sight of. It goes hiding in the belly of King Kong. Think of that beautiful girl or beautiful boy as Excalibur locked in stone and think of the real you as King Arthur, the only one that could release the magical sword from its stony prison.

The biggest question I hear you asking concerns your rock solid belief in cause and effect. The chicken is the cause of the egg, but the egg is also the cause of the chicken. Your belief in the "theory" of evolution leads you to pose the question in the first place, "what came first, the chicken or the egg?" It never occurs to you that the element of time needs to be thought about differently. You believe without doubt that you react to your environment and rarely if ever consider that your environment reacts to you. That is because you believe without doubt that your outer world of matter and stuff preexists what you believe about it and that **IT** is literal. Combined with those beliefs is the one that says what you feel and think about the outer world is the subjective non-literal. What you have read in my book says just the opposite.

It appears to you that your feelings, which are signals, follows what you believe caused them. The reality, as I have pointed out, is that they arise mutually in time. If time moved any slower in your reality your individual life would not have any movement. It would appear to you as though you were viewing an individual frame on a roll of film. When I arrived here, which is as close to you as your own skin, I saw my life as if captured in a roll of film, with each moment captured in a single frame. I understood immediately that one moment was an eternity in and of itself and that cause and effect was nothing more than a belief I held as a truth. I saw that each emotion and the physical abstract representation of it rested in a single frame of the film. A stubbed toe did not appear in one frame and my experience of pain in the next. They arise mutually and appear in the same frame. You create your own film, and as stated previously, each frame represents an individual belief. The following frame can be different for you by changing the belief that feeds your perception.

Some of you hold the belief that a diagnosis of cancer is a death sentence, even though you have seen the evidence that many 'survive' cancer. The truth is that you can be cancer free in the very next moment. You can't think it away, but you can believe it away. This is the way your reality works. In a very real sense you have all become victims of your own beliefs. None of you are victims of your outer reality, for it is you that creates it. You are not cured by your doctor or by medicines. You are cured by what you believe about your doctors and medicines. My admonition then, is to work on those beliefs that do not serve you. Throughout the history of the human race you have been under the hypnotic spell of your beliefs. One of your favorite phrases is "shit happens." Within the next fifty years you will all be saying, "my beliefs happen." It will be then that you will have reclaimed your power.

Expectations

Your misuse of expectations, regardless of your filter set, is devastating to your desires. Each moment, being a snapshot of your beliefs that wrap themselves around your process, is what keeps you from creating the next moment differently from what you expect it to be. When the process goes counter to your expectations it creates doubt and therefore diminishes trust in acquiring your desire. Doubt weakens the power of the active belief. Your entire world is interconnected and therefore cooperative. You will always draw to your experience what it is you believe. The stronger the belief the more likely you will meet your desire or goal. But, because you all have expectations regarding the process the belief is weakened when the process does not conform to your expectations. My father trusted that tree would fall where he wanted it to fall. When the tree bound up his saw as it began to fall in a different direction from where he wanted it to fall he merely borrowed his neighbor's saw to free his own. He made the cut and the tree still fell where he wanted it to. Had the tree not

The Horse Rode Me

bound his saw it would not have fallen where he wanted it to. He kept his focus on his desire rather than the process, which veered from what he expected. Yes, he was momentarily frustrated, but recognized his frustration for what it was, an emotional signal, and not a cause and effect.

Let's say you want to get sober. You have a trunk full of beliefs that establish what the process should look like, none of them suggesting it will be a breeze. Dope sickness, discomfort, struggle and urges are but a few and all of which you will probably experience. This is what focusing on the process will look like. It keeps you and many others from delaying the day you finally decide to get help. What I am suggesting is a near total focus on your desire for sobriety, which, by the way, begins its journey to you the moment you set the desire. Completely drop your expectations of the process, which is loaded with your negative beliefs. By doing so your process may wind up being completely different than your initial expectation. In this way you allow your desire for sobriety to join you unencumbered by the beliefs you held about the process. You always draw what it is you believe.

In 1980 my father was preparing for his second Boston Marathon. He was thirty-five years old, running 70 miles a week, and in the best shape of his life. His goal was to run under 2:30 for the 26.2 mile race. Six weeks before the marathon he was running 6 one mile repeats at a 5 minute per mile pace on the old UConn fieldhouse indoor 200 yard track. Rounding the last turn of his fifth mile he tore a segment of his calf muscle and went down hard. This, of course, demolished what the process to his goal should look like. Only for a moment did doubt creep in. That same day he scheduled weekly sessions of deep muscle massage with the best sports physical therapy group in Hartford, Connecticut. It was two weeks before he could run again. He felt great on race day and the conditions were perfect for a good race. Many years later when I was running cross country in middle school he told me the story I'm sharing here. He said at 23 miles he knew he was crushing his goal and felt as good at 23 as he did at 10 miles. He was overwhelmed with a vast emotion of joy that brought him to tears. "David," he said, "that moment was absolutely sublime. I felt I was in a state of grace." He went on to run a 2:25:16 a PR of over four minutes. He put together 26.2 mile repeats at a 5:32 pace. All this took place five years before he began his individual metamorphosis and discovered the information you are reading here. The point of my father's story is that he held on to his desired goal by ignoring that the process to it went completely off the expected rails.

In my Father's story he was pushing his body beyond his body's ability to respond (a belief in itself). He did not listen to the subtle signs his body was giving him. He needed to back off and rest, but ignored the soft whispering voice. After several attempts to get his attention his body took out the sledgehammer. His goal of going under a 2:30 marathon was still achievable, but only if he ignored what shape the process "should" look like. If he had followed the normal course you all take of realizing a torn calf muscle six weeks before the marathon dooms your goal, he would never have had the race of his life. He probably would not have raced at all. Instead of pushing himself on those 6 one-mile repeats, he should have been resting. He created the mechanism (unconsciously) that forced him to rest. It was the torn calf that allowed him to reach his goal. You might argue that had he not torn his calf he would have run even faster. No. He would have faced race day flat, tired and worn. This is a perfect example of setting a desire, knowing it is on the way, then letting go of your expectations of what form the process will take. This is trust, regardless of the twists and turns of the process.

The Horse Rode Me

ONE

I cannot talk about your literal connection to all things without addressing your concept of God. How you imagine God determines the boundaries you place, not only around yourselves and your beliefs, but also around reality itself. Your view of reality can be determined by the size of the God each of you envisions. Religion is a belief system not a truth. It was invented by you to remind you of You, the big You. Instead you imagined a God separate from you that looked more like the big You than God itself, who is beyond any of your imaginings. God is beyond thought, but not beyond feeling. God is the sum of all of your personalities...and more. God is the Net of Gems and more. To feel and experience your interconnectedness to all things you must give up your Idea of God to God. Killing each other over whose idea of God is the right God makes **you** weep. You see it in the eyes of weeping children that have lost their parents to war and hatred, and you see it in the eyes of parents that have lost their children. What you are seeing is God weeping, for God is the Sum of all consciousness.

The Horse Rode Me

Your understanding of God is evolving, just as your understanding of yourselves is evolving. Your current understanding of yourselves has already surpassed your understanding of the Old Testament God, Yahweh. He was a God of love, as well as a God of punishment and retribution. However, some of you still believe in a God of retribution, and even the God of retribution is God, for, as I just stated, God is the sum of all consciousness. But, there is a story that many of you attribute to God, and that is the creation of the universe that you know. That story is evolving as well. It is evolving to suggest that free will is more than you have heretofore suspected. Free will is your unobstructed freedom to manifest any belief you choose.

That you can create the life you want requires trust. Trust, however, is built over time and through a deep understanding of your own spiritual nature. Trust is a lack of doubt as I stated before. In painting a vastly larger picture of God and of yourselves I hope to lead you toward the development of trust that is a critical ingredient in creating the life you desire.

You do not believe as the late priest/philosopher, Alan Watts, does that you are one of an infinite number of divine manifestations, while at the same time part of a unified whole. Watts believed in the power of free will. Some Church dogmas state that you are a tainted creation of the divine, whose purpose is to lift you to a higher plane of spiritual existence. Some of you profess to no longer believing in God, but hold to a purely scientific belief system. You are a mere manufacturing coincidence of a mindless machine and everything goes dark when you 'die.' Those that believe in God readily admit your understanding of his nature is limited, and so what you do not understand you assign to God's 'mysterious ways'. Bad things happening to good people falls into this category, and so does good things happening to 'bad' people.

The early Gnostics defined spiritual as *'gnosis'*, or knowing.

Those without gnosis worshiped the creator and believed Christ would save them from sin. The uninitiated accepted Christ by faith, understanding neither his true nature or their own. Those who had acquired gnosis understood Christ as sent by the Father of Truth and that their nature was identical to his and to God's. This is a critical point in that it gets at the deeply rooted belief most of you still cling to, and that is that God and you are separate.

God One
For several thousand years you have been among the uninitiated, imagining for yourselves a God separate from you and whose nature is unlike your own. It could be no other way, for you were playing by the rules of your game that remained in place until the beginning of the twentieth century. Let's call the God that won-out over the God of gnosis, God One.

God One is the God most of you know, the God you created under the old rules of your game, which included a veil of forgetfulness. The Bible begins with Genesis and before time. Science begins with the big bang, which was the beginning of time. Time is significant because it underscores your inner knowing that time only relates to your physical reality, one of many. Of note is science's current quest for the theory of everything, which would have to explain the instant of creation and before. Before the Big Bang time did not exist. Keep in mind that science is as much a belief system as is religion, regardless of science's insistence that their discoveries are facts. That does not mean it is not true. It does mean that your beliefs create your truths.

The Bible doesn't tell you much, if anything, about 'before time'. What it does say is that there was 'before time.' This suggests an existence prior to your entering this world of space and time, but the problem is that the word 'before' relates to time. Science and its Big Bang theory postulates that time and space were created with one stupendous blast, but when it tries to go to 'a time' before the bang all of its mathematics breaks down. OK, let's say you are one of the many that combines a belief in God with a belief in science and the Big Bang theory. With that Bang, God One creates time and space in a single expanding universe and then waits a few billion years for the simplest form of life to appear. Reconciling Genesis in the Bible with the Big Bang is no easy task, especially if you hold to a literal interpretation of the Bible. I assume you don't or you wouldn't be reading this book.

You read the Bible as allegories rather than fact, and believing that the stories in Genesis are metaphorical you then assign God to your scientific beliefs. God created the Universe by way of the big bang. In so doing you are assigning as much a literal interpretation to the scientific mythology as do those who assign a literal interpretation to the Bible. The point I made over and over in this book is that the outer physical world of matter and experience is as much an abstract representation of your inner subjective state as are your dreams, which is not to say that it is not real. Remember the paradox.

So, let's get back to what many of you understand, which is the combining of God with the Big Bang. You are at the point in scientific explanations where the earth begins to form, some six billion years ago. God One's patience is rewarded - by himself I presume- and humans finally appear on the face of the third planet from the sun. Now, even if you hold a literal interpretation of the Bible, why would God take six days to create the world and you on it? Why wouldn't God One just pop it all into existence? Both points of view insist on time and before time. For most of human existence you have believed that the earth was the center of the universe and that you were the only form of intelligent life. You never questioned the incredible waste of space and energy involved in creating an entire universe of 100 billion galaxies, each with a 100 billion stars and then only put life forms with souls on one tiny planet. You are now not only questioning that premise, but questioning whether this is the only reality.

Keep in mind I am describing a God separate from yourselves, just as many believe him to be. Even those that believe you are one with God do not order their daily living based on that belief. For a very, very few this belief of unity has moved from concept into experience. But this book is not for them. Anyway, being able to see all things, God One watches all of you grow and die, with all of the drama you can muster in-between. God One never told you, but he has given you the power of creation. Things never just happened to you. God One just never gave you the rules by which you were to play your physical game. He made you forget you were him and yourselves at the same time. And so, having forgot, you became victims and assigned God his mysterious ways for the things you could not understand. You knew God One was love and so you had to explain some pretty horrific events by giving yourselves a nature that just couldn't comprehend the nature of God and was different than his. Remember, God One is a reflection of your own understanding of yourselves and not the other way around.

You have created your image of God as needing your help in so many ways. Well, he doesn't need your help, but many of you think he does. One would think that the real God could do for himself what you seem to think he needs you to do on his behalf. If he needed more devotees why doesn't he just create them? Wouldn't you rather he do it in a flash than have all those missionaries and evangelists proselytizing around the globe. Free will, you say. Ah ha! There's the rub. You either have free will to create all of your experience or you don't. I want to get you to the point where you trust that you do create it all, while not losing your knowing connection to a loving God.

I invite you to think long and hard about this God One, for in many ways he is much like yourselves. In fact, many of you live your lives far more compassionately than your conception of God One does. There are many that live the life of the Old Testament God. Yahweh was definitely a hard-love kind of guy, and many today rebel against his types of actions. Caligula would have loved the Old Testament God as he was much like him; although a little heavy on the retribution side.

Let's get literal. For example, if you were an all-powerful creator God of love and light and found yourself needing some companionship, would you take a few billion years, or even six days to do it? It sounds more like something you would do, based on your beliefs about time, than the real God would do. If you could do anything you wanted, why not pop it all into existence at once? And if God really loved you beyond the depths that you can conceive of love, wouldn't he give you the same powers as himself; the power to create whatever life you desired? So, get rid of the old, 'his ways are mysterious' as an explanation for the horrendous things that happen to you that you can't make any sense of. Get the monkey off of God One's back and put it on your own. You can never get it off unless you realize it is on your back and not on God's.

If you were God One wouldn't you rather participate in your creation rather than watch it? Personally, I'd rather be in a movie than watch one. Wouldn't the experience be richer if you actually became your creation, while at the same time allowing them all the autonomy to create their own realities? In order to do this, however, God One would have to install a veil of forgetfulness so that each of you doesn't remember their God connection. The veil was simply part of the game rules you all agreed upon.

Thank You, Jesus
Thanking God is polite, a little like thanking the waitress for good service, but it wasn't the waitress that made the meal possible. It was your money that paid for it. You see those in the limelight thanking God all the time for their success. What you don't see is the individual acknowledging themselves. That would be hubris, a very strong religious belief. Sweden actually has a law against flaunting what you have. God forbid you should cross that religious line that says 'stay small', 'stay humble'.

Might not God be a little more complex than the image you have mustered? Or, have you created God in your own image? Sounds a little like it to me from my current vantage point. Do you wish for your children that they go unseen in the world, or do you wish greatness for them, or at the least equanimity? If you wish greatness for your children then why do you bombard them with the conflicting message that having a big ego will bring trouble? Having said all this, there is nothing wrong with your current concept of God if individually you always get what you want and your lives flow forward, conflict free. So, If you like your current conception of God and your image serves you, keep it. But, why can you, who believe you are so much less than God One, conceive of a larger image of God than your God One has created for himself? It seems credible to think that if you can conceive of a larger God, so could the real God. I will tell you that pain and suffering is not your lot and if your understanding of suffering is that it is God's will, then I invite you to take a look at a more complex God, the God you are in the process of reimagining. I invite you to imagine along with me a larger God Two, while keeping in mind the possibility that you have created God One in your image. You may now be creating a larger God Two in the same way, as a new rule is inserted into your game of physical reality; the lifting of the veil.

God Two
God Two is really gender neutral, but calling God 'It' doesn't seem right. My sensing is that your new creation of God Two is more feminine in energy than God One, so I'm going to switch to the feminine pronoun. Several thousand years of personalizing your Gods has formed strong habits, and old habits die hard. God Two is the personification of energy and movement, and as such she does not want to wait around watching paint dry, or watching you perform your individual dramas. There are those of you that live your lives for and through your children, but your general thinking on that matter is that the parents need to get their own life. God Two wants to be her creations and herself at the same time. Keep in mind, that God Two represents your own growing

understanding of your true natures.

So, how does God Two do this? She unfolds herself, for lack of a better word, into an infinite number of forms and realities. To make the game more interesting God Two in the beginning decides to forget, at least temporarily, that each form in your reality is its own self and herself at the same time. The forgetting makes the experience more rich and fulfilling (fulfilling does not necessarily mean good) for each form. I am speaking only of God Two in your reality. As you may suspect, there are numberless realities.

God Two wants to experience all that there is to experience, but to do that she adds a little twist. She wants to experience everything as you, since your personality will experience differently the same events everyone else experiences. No two experiences are alike. But, God Two wants even more than that. She wants to experience every probability (Quantum Mechanics lends a clue here). She wants to experience both the roads taken and not taken. So, whenever there is a significant choice to be made, like do you become a doctor or an artist, God Two experiences both choices. She does this by creating another you at every significant crossroad. Keep in mind that She is actually You. From my current location we call these other selves of you probable selves, and they are as real in their parallel realities are you are in yours. They experience life exactly as you have up until the crossroad, and there are countless crossroads. The probable self, as real as the you that you see in the mirror and with the same Split Jeans, will then create its own probable selves. God Two does not mess around with creating experiences for herself. She does this by slipping into one of the infinite number of universes she has created within the same space. Impossible? Only if your god is God One. Remember, if you can imagine it, so can God Two. Your Physicists are already postulating an infinite number of universes in order to accommodate their theories.

With God Two there are many 'yous', each as real and as independent as the 'you' reading these words and all interacting with and influencing each other in subtle ways. In this way God Two gets to experience it all, at least as much as your imagination can conceive of. But, it is more than just experience, for without creation there would be nothing to experience. Experience becomes a by-product of creation, and God Two is a hands-on kind of God. You'll never hear of God Two being called a couch potato. She unfolds and enfolds herself infinitely in a spacious present, for there is only the present. Many religions refer to it as eternity. God Two is the creator God to beat all creator Gods. But, she creates out of herself, unlike God One, who seemingly creates with a magic wand or finger, and whose creations, you have believed, are separate from him. What is the purpose of God One's creations if they are separate from him? Toys to play with, maybe? No!

God Two goes further yet. She endows her creations of herself with their own ability to create. It's called free will and it is like a chain reaction of creations, but with a kicker. Since you have forgotten until now that you are all individual manifestations of God Two, you cannot conceive of being the sole responsible party for the creation of your lives. This is where all these 'thank you God' proclamations come in. But, because you are the responsible party and since you have experienced all you can experience under the veil of forgetfulness, you are moving on. You are slowly lifting the veil of what my father referred to as The Forgotten Self, and are in the process of inserting new game rules into your version of physical reality. Your power is immense, and creating on autopilot has grown tiresome to who you really are. Consciousness demands movement and change, and so you are now in the grip of a shift in consciousness, or better said, a shift in the game rules of this particular reality. With the forgotten self sometimes you pinned the tail on the donkey's ass and sometimes you missed. In drug addiction you miss the entire donkey. As the shift unfolds you will be gradually lifting the blindfold. You will always put that tail where it belongs because you will have remembered who you are and what the new rules of the game are. You will no longer feel the need to say, "thank you Lord," for you will know that it was you that pinned that tail squarely above the Donkey's ass.

A belief in God Two and an overthrow of your concept of God One would result in the unexplained being explained. It would explain why bad things happen to good people. All things happen to all people and all probable selves for the mere experience of it. Behind all your faces is the face of God, but your faces are also your own. You are Russian Matryoshka dolls, where inside the largest doll is a smaller one, and inside the smaller one is yet another. And on and on it goes.

You have not been good at accepting responsibility for yourselves because your attention has been outside yourselves. It was either, "the devil made me do it," or it was "thank you Jesus." Things happen to you, and others are the cause of how you feel. Many times you assign blame or responsibility to God. That kind of thinking lets you off the hook as you continue to play the game of victim without knowing the rules, but it keeps the monkey on your back. So, you have words like 'accident' and 'coincidence' and 'bad luck' and 'good luck'. With God Two you hold yourselves accountable for everything, and in so doing redefine 'good' and 'bad'. They are merely a choice of preferences. Your world has not been forced upon you. It is you that has chosen.

This information represents a titanic shift, but a shift that should make sense in a world where bad things happen to both good and bad people. It explains everything. Good and bad become less things-that-happen-to-you, and more things-you-create-in-alignment-your-own-Intent and Exploration. The mythologist Joseph Campbell once said that when looking back on his life he has found that what seemed so black and defeating at the time, ultimately turned out to be life-transforming. Your concept of God One throws you into a world where you react to accidents and coincidences and wail "why me?" In God One's world you are like pinballs with a mysterious God at the flippers. With God Two there is meaning and communications in everything that happens, for everything that happens is self-created and is a reflection of your inner selves' desire to fulfill its Intent. In God Two's world you are the pinballs, the pinball machine and the operator of the flippers. You are not here to reach a higher spiritual realm. You are already your highest expression of Self, whether you be sinner or saint; addict or straight. You are here to experience and expand consciousness in physical form. You are here to play, and in this sense Joseph Campbell is right. Life is a game.

Under the grand idea of God Two the world becomes a cooperative venture in consciousness, and just as your entire body feels a stubbed toe, so does every soul feel and react to a child or an adult starving to death in any part of the world. If you are all connected, all individual manifestations of the divine, then you must all feel it in some way and have affected it in some way. Not only that, but since you have all been "God with amnesia," then nobody leaves this world before his time or by any means other than that of his or her own choosing. Until now you just haven't known it. Now, this is a pretty tough nut to swallow, particularly for most of you who have believed in the smaller God One. After all, there are some pretty horrific ways to leave your planet, and with God One you always wonder how he could allow such things to happen.

God Two is very clever, but believing in God Two does not change the fact that hitting yourself in the head with a hammer is going to hurt like hell. And why is it going to hurt like hell? Because you believe profoundly that it will hurt like hell. Telling yourself it won't hurt won't change the depth of the underlying belief and create the trust necessary to avoid head damage and pain. You do not yet trust that you can hit yourself in the head with a hammer and not have it hurt. If it is too much of a stretch to think of yourself as God, then think of yourself as a Godlet until the idea can settle in. You are God One. You have chosen to morph into God Two. Many more lay ahead of you.

The Horse Rode Me

The Horse Rode Me

Wrapping up

The choice is now up to you. Do you remain on auto-pilot, or do you wake up and take the helm of your own ship? Do you continue to punch holes in the bow of your ship while sleeping, or do you wake up and steer your ship to avoid the dangers? I've given you the sextant to plot your course consciously, but it will take time and practice to learn how to use it effectively. In your reality your beliefs are your most powerful tools, and they are quite specific. Some of you will be fast learners and will only be met by the sledge hammer occasionally, while others will continue to suffer many bumps and bruises. The difference will be that both groups will now understand that it is you that got out the sledge. Knowing that gives you the power to change what it is you do not like. Everything, and I mean everything is and always has been on your side. It will continue to give you exactly what you focus upon. Believing any other way abdicates your power, even though it is still you that wields it, albeit unconsciously.

You are at the flippers of your own pin ball game. Learn to play it the way it was meant to be played. You cannot make the shot if your Monkey Mind is focused on how you are going to afford the gas you put in your car or how you will pay your hospital bill or how you will get your next fix. Your Monkey Mind is your greatest obstacle to remaining present, and as I have told you, the present is your only place of power. Set your goal, take action and then let go of all expectations regarding the process. There is purpose in detours, but they get you to where you were planning to go if you keep your focus on your destination.

I cannot overstate the power of Appreciation in ALL of this. Practice appreciation daily. It has the power to break bad habits of thinking. Here are a few items you might want to consider appreciating: Your immune system, your organs, your senses, your friends, your enemies, YOU. Do it often. Your Monkey Mind cannot begin jabbering away when you are in the act of appreciation.

Let's not forget Acceptance, which is not fatalism. In its simplest form it means do not judge, either yourself or another. You have no idea what another is exploring. You now know that she/he/it is connected to you and is as responsive to your beliefs as you are to theirs. You can replace unconditional love with Acceptance as I have defined it previously. Acceptance does not need to include affection. Knowing and appreciation is love. Affection is different. Acceptance requires that you allow, without judgment, all differences. You don't have to be friends with red neck Billy Bob and Red Neck Billy Bob need not be friends with Snowflake William. You both, however need to accept your differences. When you do so you may just find that you have more in common than that which divides you.

What I am about to say next is likely to get every psychotherapists' panties in a bunch. You will not find the answers to what troubles you today by rummaging around in the past. What you need to rummage around in is your tool box of beliefs, and not who did this to you or that to you when you were a kid. Absolutely no one and no thing is to blame for who you are now. In fact you might all consider getting rid of the word entirely. The word itself connotes you or someone else did something that altered you. You are like the mythological King Midas whose touch transforms everything into gold. You are more magical, though. Everything you perceive turns into matter that is fully responsive to you. **WHAT COULD BE BETTER THAN THAT!**

"God himself culminates in the present moment, and will never be more divine in the lapse of all the ages. And we are enabled to apprehend at all what is sublime and noble only by the perpetual instilling and drenching of the reality that surrounds us.

The Horse Rode Me

The universe constantly and obediently answers to our conceptions; whether we travel fast or slow, the track is laid for us. Let us spend our lives conceiving them. Each humblest plant, or weed, stands there to express some thought or mood of ours, and yet how long it stands in vain! We are one virtue, one truth, one beauty. All nature is our satellite, whose light is dull and reflected. She is subaltern to us, an episode to our poem; but we are primary, and radiate light and heat to the system." **Henry David Thoreau**

I KNOW AND APPRECIATE YOU.

Addendum
For Steve and Em, and Ben and Em and Becky

I Shall be Released
By
Bob Dylan

They say everything can be replaced
They say every distance is not near
So I remember every face
Of every Man who put me here

I see my light come shinning
From the west down to the east
Any day now, any day now
I shall be released

They say every man needs protection
They say every man musty fall
So I swear I see my reflection
Somewhere inside these walls.

The Horse Rode Me

I see my light come shinning
From the west unto the east
Any day now, any day now
I shall be released

Yonder stands a man in this lonely crowd
Man who swears he's not to blame
All day long I hear him hollering so loud
Just crying out that he's not to blame

I see my light come shinning
From the west down to the east
Any day now, any day now
I shall be released.

The Horse Rode Me

Split Jeans

Made in the USA
Middletown, DE
02 June 2021